D0457564

AN INSTANT GUIDE TO

WILDFLOWERS

The most familiar species of
North American wildflowers
described and illustrated in color

Pamela Forey and Cecilia Fitzsimons

2

BONANZA BOOKS
New York

Distribution map

● Commonly found in these regions

○ Partial distribution only

First published 1986 by Bonanza Books,
distributed by Crown Publishers, Inc.

© 1986 Atlantis Publications Ltd.

Printed in Spain

ISBN 0–517–61675–0

Contents

Introduction

This is a book for those who want to be able to identify the wildflowers that they see on the roadsides or the "weeds" that grow in the back yard. Many people who do not have the time or opportunity to make a close study of them would still appreciate some means of easily identifying a flower that catches their eye along the road, in the yard, or even on waste ground or in a National Park. We have selected from the thousands of North American flowering plants those species most likely to be encountered in the countryside of the more heavily populated areas of the United States and Canada. The names of the plants used here are those commonly used in reference books, but you may know them under other more local names. You need not assume that you have identified them wrongly if you do not recognize the name. Many of the most common wildflowers have been introduced from Europe and this has been indicated in the text where relevant.

How to use this book

We have divided the book into sections on the basis of flower color, to make it as easy as possible for you to find your flower quickly. However flowers do not always obey man-made rules. Even within a single species the flowers may range in color from white to pink or mauve. It is also not always easy to tell exactly what color a flower is — whether it is palest pink or white, for instance. The book is divided into six basic sections on the basis of flower color; **White**, **Yellow and Orange**, **Green**, **Blue and Purple**, **Red and Pink**, and **Variable**. Most of the flowers that you encounter will belong to the first five sections and you should be able to decide which section each belongs to quite easily. However, if you have a palest pink flower it might be worth while looking in both the pink and the white sections.

The last section contains flower groups like asters and milkweeds which have a wide variation in their flower color. Fortunately there are not many flower groups like this and so the section is quite short. It will only be necessary to use it if you have not found your flower in your original choice of color section.

It is possible you will not be able to find your exact plant in this book for there are thousands of wildflowers in North America. However we have included the majority of the familiar plants as well as examples of all the major families and genera, so that you should be able to find one similar if not the same.

Guide to identification

First decide to which color section your flower belongs. You will then find that each section is further subdivided by habitat — the place where the plant is growing — indicated by the symbol at the top of the page. There are three major habitat divisions indicated by these symbols. Most of the plants grow in one or other of these habitats, but a few cross the boundaries and such plants have a combined symbol at the top of the page. Groups of plants, like asters, that grow in all three have a fourth symbol. (See Fig. 1)

Fig. 1 Key to habitats

Man-made habitats
Roadsides: waste ground: cultivated land: fields.

Dry natural habitats
Prairies and dry grassland: dry open woods: dry open or stony ground: sagebrush and other scrub: deserts: rocky areas.

Moist or wet natural habitats
Wet meadows and marshes: water margins: ponds and lakes: moist shady woods: wet rocks.

All three habitats

The habitat classification is designed to help you confirm your identification of a flower. If you are in a dry open picnic area in open grassland, then you are only likely to find those flowering plants designated as growing in dry open grassland or on sandy or stony ground. Plants designated as growing in moist shady woods or in wet meadows and marshes, for instance, can be eliminated.

Characteristics of your plant
Plants can rarely be identified by a single feature. It is usually the combination of flower type, flower arrangement, leaf shape and leaf arrangement that tells you that this is the right plant. The first two boxes in the text description are designed to give you this information. Confirmation that this plant is found in the right habitat and in your part of North America is given in the third box and a distribution map is provided for quick reference. Finally the fourth box gives you a more

9

general description of the group of plants to which this one belongs and indicates some of the similar species with which it might be confused.

Flowers and fruits
Information about the flowers and fruits includes the way in which the flowers grow, singly or in clusters for instance, their shape, number of petals and any peculiarities etc.; the type of fruit produced is also included, with further details if these are of particular interest in this plant. Flowering times are given at the bottom of the page. They vary with distribution and abbreviations (see Fig. 2) have been given to indicate this variation before the relevant months.

General form of the plant
The second box contains a more general description of the plant, with some indication of its size, its habit (whether it forms clumps or spreading mats, etc.), its leaf arrangement and leaf shape.

Habitat and distribution
Because of the wide variation in climate and geography in North America, the area and habitat in which a flowering plant may be found are important clues to its identity. Many of the plants in this book fall into three groups, those found in the east, those found in the midwestern prairies and those found west of the Rocky mountains. The distribution of the plant is given in the map and more detailed information is given in the distribution box so that you can see at a glance whether you might expect to find the plant wild in your part of North America. It should be noted however, that the plant may not be common, or even present, throughout the whole of the area and may also be introduced elsewhere as a garden plant, as an escape from cultivation or as a weed.

Flower groups
The vast majority of flower species are part of a group of related plants called a genus (plural "genera"). Genera are in turn grouped together into families. In the final box we have generally given brief descriptions of one or two members of the same genus or family as the featured plant. They are usually the most similar and most likely to be confused with the plant illustrated. Where the plants are illustrated in another part of the book their names appear in bold print. Where there are many similar species in a genus, many of which are common, like the asters or the goldenrods, we have given a generic description throughout; most of the plants in the variable color section are of this type.

Other common species
At the end of several of the sections you will find pages of other common species. These are mostly less widespread than the featured plants or less likely to be encountered. However several of them, especially members of the daisy family, are common plants similar to species featured in the main part of the book.

Now you are ready to use this book. It is designed to fit in your pocket, so take it with you on your next trip and don't forget to check your sightings on the check-list provided with the index. Remember that wildflowers are becoming ever rarer in our country so please do not dig them up or pick them. Rare species are protected by Federal and State laws which are often strictly enforced. Photographing the flowers where they are growing provides a lasting alternative which is becoming more and more popular.

Fig. 2 Specimen page

Color of band denotes color of flower(s)

Name of plant

Symbol of habitat type (Fig. 1)

Name(s) of species illustrated if a group description

Distribution map

Color illustration of characteristics

Inset species, related to featured plant

Characteristics of flowers and fruit

General description of plant

Typical habitat and distribution

Description of genus and/or related species

Flowering period. (P) Pacific states (N) north (S) south

GROUNDSEL
Golden Butterweed (1)

Flower heads formed only of yellow tubular florets, almost enclosed in a "cup" of green bracts; borne in small clusters in the axils of the upper leaves. Seeds spindle-shaped, with many long white hairs and blow freely in the wind.

A small annual weed with a branched stem, up to one foot tall. Leaves are irregularly toothed, may be cottony and the upper ones have clasping bases; they are alternately arranged.

Found in waste places, on roadsides and as a weed of cultivated ground throughout the USA and Canada. European alien.

The related native Butterweeds and Ragworts may have similar flower heads to Groundsel or may have ray florets around the outside of the head. Many grow in wet meadows and woods. Golden Butterweed (inset) has heart-shaped leaves and grows in wet meadows and woods in eastern USA and Canada.

Flowering period: Throughout most of the year.

11

Glossary

Annual A plant which grows from a seed, flowers, sets seed and dies in one year.

Biennial A plant which forms leaves in the first year, produces a flowering shoot in the second year, flowers, sets seed and dies.

Perennial A plant which lives from year to year, starting into growth again each spring.

Node A point on a stem at which the leaves are produced. On a creeping stem roots may also be produced at this point.

Succulent Crisp and juicy or soft and juicy.

Flower Structure

- corolla
- calyx
- stamen
- stigma
- petal
- receptacle
- ovary ⎱ fruit
- seeds ⎰
- sepal
- bract
- reflexed sepal

Flower Types

male — stamens only

female — ovaries only

orchid

spurred

pea-like

two-lipped or hooded

disk florets

daisy

ray florets

Flower Arrangement

umbel

cluster

spike

spray

Leaf Types

simple leaves — not divided into leaflets

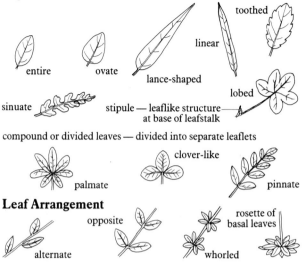

compound or divided leaves — divided into separate leaflets

Leaf Arrangement

Fruits

Berry A juicy fruit which contains several seeds.

Capsule A dry fruit, usually rounded and containing one to several sections and many seeds. It may split open down the sides or at the top or bottom to release the seeds or it may have developed holes through which the seeds escape.

Nutlet A hard dry fruit containing a single seed. In some plant families, like the mint and borage families, the nutlets develop in groups of four.

Pod A long dry fruit, usually containing several large seeds, which splits open along one or both seams to release the seeds.

Vegetative structures

Bulb A very short underground stem with many swollen leaves growing from it, forming a foodstore for next year's plant.

Corm A swollen, underground, food-storing stem, formed at the base of the leaves and on top of last year's corm.

Offshoot A new plant formed on a short creeping stem which grows from the parent plant. Often many offshoots are formed so that the original plant may be ringed by "babies".

Runner A long creeping stem growing from a parent plant, on which new plants form at the nodes.

Field Chickweed (1), Common Chickweed (2)

Flowers in loose branching clusters. The five white petals may be so deeply divided that there appear to be ten and they alternate with the sepals. Fruits are capsules, cupped in the calyx and opening by teeth.

Small annual or perennial plants, often forming an untidy mat or clump with many weak leafy shoots which bear terminal flowers; leaves mostly opposite and lance-shaped or linear. Some are sticky to the touch.

Common weeds of grassland, roadsides and waste places throughout much of the USA and Canada. Other species grow in woodland. Many are European aliens.

Amongst the most common are Field Chickweed and Mouse-ear Chickweed, both small matted plants with hairy stems and leaves. Mouse-ear Chickweed has very small petals. Common Chickweed is larger with terminal clusters of flowers; both the latter have five very deeply divided petals.

Flowering period: April–frost.

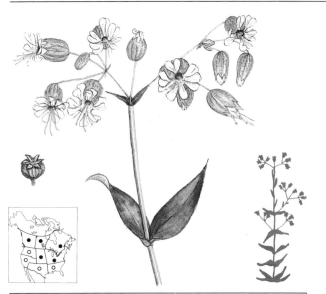

Flowers borne in loose clusters at the tops of the stems. The tubular section of the white corolla is partially enclosed in a distinctive bladder-like calyx. Fruits are globular capsules enclosed in persistent calyx.

A perennial plant with several weakly erect, more or less hairless, stems, up to 18in. high. Each stem bears several opposite pairs of lance-shaped leaves, the uppermost of which clasp the stem.

Found on roadsides, in fields and waste places throughout the USA and southern Canada. Rare in the Pacific states and not common in the south.

One of many Campions (or Catchflys). Their flowers often open in the afternoon or evening. They are distinguished from each other by flower shape and color (some have red flowers) and leaf arrangement. Similar species include Sleepy Catchfly and Starry Catchfly.

Flowering period: April–August.

Flowers borne in small erect spikes, individually very small with four white, spoon-shaped petals. Fruits are characteristically purse-shaped pods, like little hearts, borne on long stalks.

A small annual weed, often only 6in. tall, with a rosette of basal leaves, each tapering towards the base and often deeply toothed and somewhat hairy. Leaves on flower stalk have clasping bases.

A small but distinctive plant found in waste ground, back yards, roadsides and fields throughout the USA and much of Canada. European alien.

Peppergrasses are somewhat larger rougher plants with rounder pods, and in some species the pods are narrowly winged. Field Pennycresses are also larger than Shepherd's Purse and have flattened, round, winged pods with a deep notch at the top.

Flowering period: Often throughout the year.

CLEAVERS

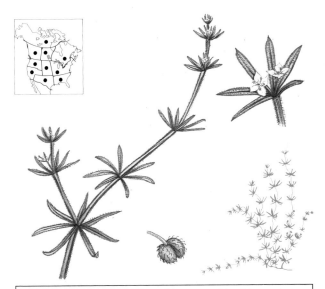

Tiny tubular flowers, with four white or greenish-white petals, are borne in small clusters in the axils of the uppermost leaves. Fruits distinctive, borne in pairs, each one small, rounded and covered in hooks.

A scrambling annual plant forming clumps of lax stems supported by other vegetation. The four-angled stems bear hooked bristles on the angles and the linear bristly leaves are arranged in whorls of six or eight.

Found in thickets, moist shady woodland and waste places throughout the USA and Canada, except the extreme north.

This is one of many species of Bedstraws, but Cleavers is rather larger than most. The majority are small, profusely branched plants with leaves in whorls and white or yellow flowers borne in small clusters. Some species smell of new-mown hay.

Flowering period: July–September. (P) March–July.

Many tiny white flowers borne in tight umbels, often with one purple flower in the center, and 7–13 three-forked bracts beneath the umbel. In "fruit" the umbel becomes cup-like, like a bird's nest and contains spiky fruits.

A biennial plant forming a rosette of ferny leaves in the first year. The flowering stem of the following year is ribbed and coarsely hairy, up to 3ft. tall, with finely divided leaves. The plant smells of carrots.

Found in open dry places, roadsides and waste ground throughout the USA and southern Canada. European alien.

A member of the large carrot family, all with the typical umbels of flowers, in white or yellow. White-flowered species include the poisonous Hemlock, with purple-spotted stems and fetid odor; Water Parsnip which grows in wet places; and the herbs Caraway and Coriander.

Flowering period: April–September.

COMMON NIGHTSHADE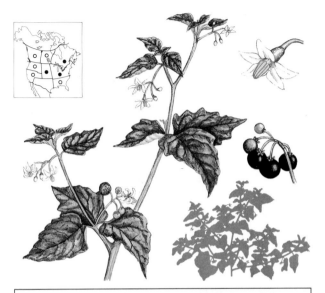

Flowers borne in small clusters on long stalks in the leaf axils; petals five, fused into a tube and with five protruding yellow anthers. Fruits are poisonous berries, green at first, turning black when ripe.

A sprawling annual plant with one main branched green stem, up to 12in. high. Leaves alternate, rhomboid in shape, dull green, more or less hairless.

A weed of cultivated ground and waste places, found throughout much of Canada and the USA but rare in the south and in desert areas. European alien.

Other common or widespread Nightshade species include Bittersweet, a scrambling plant with purple petals and yellow anthers; White Nightshade, a Californian weed with white, purple-tinged petals; and Wild Tomato, a prairie species with white flowers.

Flowering period: May–frost.

⌂ COMMON MALLOW

Flowers borne in small sprays in leaf axils. Petals five, notched, white with lilac veins, and widely separated from each other. Fruits of Mallows are distinctive, like bristly segmented cheeses enclosed in persistent calyx.

A sprawling annual plant up to 3ft. tall, with tough downy stems and rounded, often lobed leaves borne on long stalks. There are conspicuous stipules at the bases of the leaf stalks.

Found in waste places, on roadsides and on cultivated ground throughout the USA and southern Canada. European alien.

Other Mallows likely to be encountered are Musk Mallow with deeply divided stem leaves and larger pink flowers; and Common Mallow with purple flowers. Small-flowered Mallow has very small pale pink flowers, almost enclosed in the sepals. Superficially similar **Cranesbills** have distinctive fruits.

Flowering period: April–frost.

Flowers borne in long drooping sprays in the axils of the leaves. The flowers have no petals but the five sepals are whitish green instead. Fruits are purple black berries borne in long sprays.

A leafy, clump-forming, perennial plant, up to 9ft. tall, strong-smelling and hairless, with several reddish stems and many large, alternate, lance-shaped leaves.

Found in waste places, on roadsides and on cultivated ground, in southern Canada and eastern and southern USA.

No similar species.

Flowering period: May–frost.

21

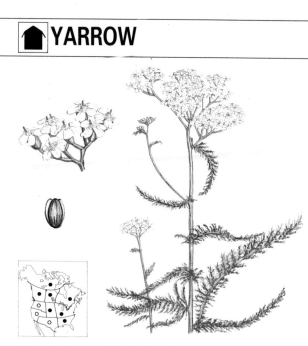

Flowers white or pink-tinged, borne in large flat clusters, on top of the erect stems. Each flower head looks like a single flower but actually has five outer ray florets and a central disk of tubular florets. Seeds have small wings.

A creeping perennial plant with many woolly erect stems, often only 12in. high, bearing soft, deep green feathery leaves and terminal flower heads. The plant has a distinctive scent.

Found on roadsides and in grassland throughout the USA and most of Canada, except the far north. Both native and European forms are present.

Yarrow is unlikely to be confused with other members of the daisy family except maybe Sneezeweed Yarrow, an eastern species which has simple, narrow leaves and larger flowers; or with the taller Thoroughworts which have large, simple, opposite leaves and flowers in fuzzy heads.

Flowering period: June–August. (P) March–November.

Flower heads large and solitary, up to 2in. across, with an outer circle of overlapping, long white ray florets and a central yellow disk; borne terminally on long stalks. Seeds are pale gray and hairless.

A perennial plant with basal rosettes of long-stalked, spoon-shaped, toothed leaves and erect stalks, up to 3ft. tall, with lobed or toothed, clasping leaves and solitary flower heads.

Found on roadsides, in meadows and fields throughout Canada and the USA except for central southern areas. European alien.

Several other daisies are common and widespread, including the Chamomiles and Mayweeds. These have deeply lobed or lacy leaves and bear their flowers in clusters, in contrast to the Ox-eye Daisy, and many of them have strong disagreeable odors.

Flowering period: June–August.

Flowers borne in small flat clusters on long stalks; small and white, like tiny roses, with five petals alternating with the sepals. Sepals joined together behind the flower. Fruits are strawberries, with seeds on the surface.

A small, perennial, clump-forming plant with tufts of long-stalked, hairy leaves, each with three toothed leaflets. It forms several runners — thin, prostrate stems which root at the nodes to form new plants.

Found in open woods, on woodland edges and in grassland throughout the USA and southern Canada, but commoner at higher altitudes in south.

Wild Strawberries are only likely to be mistaken for Mock Strawberry which has similar, but tasteless, fruit and yellow flowers. No other plants bear strawberries. **Rough Cinquefoil** has similar leaves but is larger, has yellow flowers and does not have strawberries.

Flowers: April–June. Fruits: June–July.

NODDING ONION ☀

Wild Garlic (1)

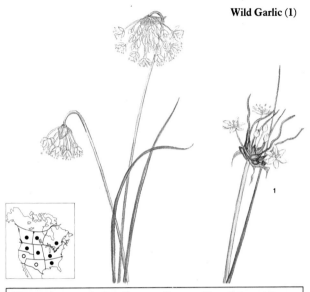

Flowers borne on leafless flower stalk, up to 2ft. tall, in nodding umbel. Individual flowers have six white or pink petals. They droop at first, becoming erect as they age and the capsules which follow are also held erect.

A bulbous plant with a reddish purple bulb, covered with a membranous coat, from which grows a clump of thin, flattened grass-like leaves and several flower stalks. The whole plant smells of onions.

Found in open woodland, rocky slopes, prairies and dry meadows throughout southern Canada and the USA except Calif.

There are very many Onion species in N. America but this is probably the most common. Some, like Wild Garlic (inset), produce bulbils as well as flowers in their umbels; other widespread species are Wild Leek with broad leaves; and Wild Chives with soft, hollow leaves.

Flowering period: July–August.

☀ SEGO LILY

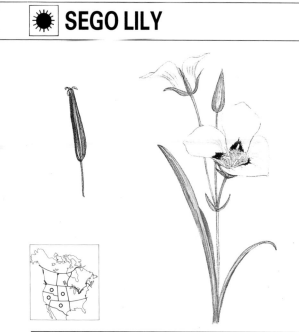

Flowers tulip-like with three petals, white with a yellow spot below a red horse-shoe mark inside at the base of each petal; one to four are borne on long stalks in a cluster at the top of the stem. Fruit an erect, lance-shaped capsule.

A perennial plant, growing from a corm. It has a single erect stem, up to 15in. tall, with several linear leaves, which become smaller nearer to the top of the stem. A small bulb is often present in the axil of the lowermost leaf.

Found on dry open slopes and in desert areas in central and western USA.

This is one of the Mariposa Tulips and the most widespread, the majority being found in southwestern USA. They may have white, yellow or pink flowers and are distinguished one from another by the markings in the flowers. The Star Tulips have pointed petals.

Flowering period: May–August.

SPANISH BAYONET ☀

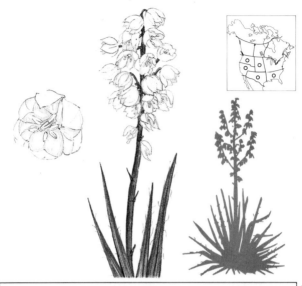

Flowers usually creamy or greenish white, like drooping waxen bells; borne in large flower spikes, up to 10ft. tall, growing from the center of the rosette. Fruits are fleshy edible berries.

A large perennial plant with a woody base from which grow one or more rosettes of stiff, sharply pointed, slightly rolled, linear leaves, up to 4ft. tall. The leaves have sheathing bases and in some species have fibrous edges.

Found on dry hillsides and in scrub in the west, on dunes, in sandy ground and in brackish marshes in the east, all but one species in southern areas of the USA.

Spanish Bayonet plants or Yuccas mostly have whitish flowers but one widespread southern species has blooms which are reddish brown on the outside and cream inside. Only one species is found outside the south (illustrated) and this spreads throughout central and western USA into Canada.

Flowering period: May–August.

Fendler's Waterleaf (1)

Flowers white or pale lilac, bell-shaped, with petals split half-way down; borne in clusters, on long flower stalks, in the leaf axils. Stamens project a long way beyond the flower. Fruits are rounded capsules.

A perennial, clump-forming plant with stout creeping underground stems from which grow many long-stalked, divided 5–7-lobed leaves. Leaves often look as if they are stained with water.

Found in damp shady woods and beside streams in eastern and northeast USA and in eastern Canada.

Other Waterleafs found in eastern USA include Broad-leaved Waterleaf which has palmate leaves and white flowers. Pacific species include Fendler's Waterleaf (inset), and Dwarf Waterleaf with divided leaves and flower clusters on very short stalks.

Flowering period: May–August.

FALSE SOLOMON'S-SEAL

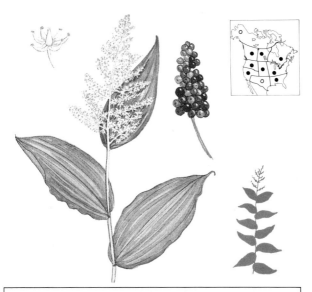

Flowers small and white, fragrant, crowded into branched clusters at the tops of the arching stems. Each flower has six petals. Fruits are clusters of small berries, turning red when ripe.

A perennial plant with slowly spreading roots, from which grow arching stems, up to 3ft. tall. Leaves are large, oval in shape with pointed tips, arranged alternately on the stems.

Found in moist shady woodland throughout the USA and southern Canada, in mountain areas in the south.

Starry False Solomon's-seal is just as widespread but less common in the south. Its leaves are arranged in a close zig-zag along the stem. True Solomon's-seals have small bell-like flowers in the leaf axils of all the leaves.

Flowering period: April–June. (P) March–May.

:·LADIES' TRESSES

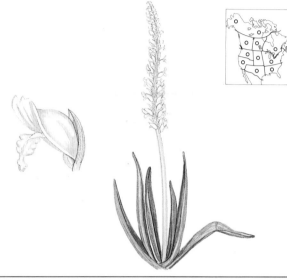

Many fragrant, white flowers are borne in three rows on a twisted flowering stem. Each has four white "petals" forming a hood and a white, green-streaked lip. Fruit is a capsule.

A perennial plant with a single thick, erect flowering shoot, up to 18in. tall, bearing many lance-shaped leaves near the base. Upper leaves much smaller than lower ones, with sheathing bases.

Found in moist open woods, bogs and wet meadows in southern Canada, northeastern and north central USA and further south in the Rocky Mountains.

There are many small Ladies' Tresses orchids in N. America but this is the only one at all widespread. They all have similar flower spikes but vary in the shape (many have spreading "petals" instead of hoods) and size of the flowers, and in their leaf shapes.

Flowering period: June–September.

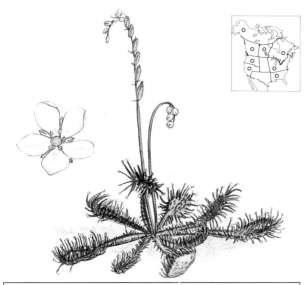

Flowers borne on slender, arching shoots, up to 9in. high, opening one or two at a time. Flowers white or tinged with pink, with five petals. Fruits are capsules with many seeds.

A small perennial, insect-eating plant which forms little rosettes of round, long-stalked leaves. The leaves are red-green in color, with many reddish, glistening, sticky hairs which act as insect traps.

Found in acid bogs and on lake margins, especially with Sphagnum moss, throughout Canada and in eastern and Pacific USA but not in southern central states.

There are several other Sundews found in similar places, differing mainly in the shape of their leaves. Pitcher Plants are also carnivorous plants of marshes and bogs, but are quite different in appearance with pitcher-shaped insect traps.

Flowering period: July–September.

⠄⠂ WATERCRESS

Flowers white with four petals, and borne in loose erect spikes. Fruits are slender pods, borne more or less upright, with the outlines of the two rows of reticulated seeds showing clearly through the "skin".

A succulent perennial plant with weak stems which lie in the water, rooting at the nodes, and then turn upwards. Erect stems bear alternate, compound, dark green leaves with characteristic peppery taste.

Found in running water, streams and springs throughout the USA. European alien. Widely grown for use in salads.

The most familiar of several Watercresses and the related Bittercresses, which grow in streams and other wet places. All have small white flowers but can be distinguished by leaf shape and differences in the shapes of the fruits.

Flowering period: April–June. (P) All year.

ARROWHEAD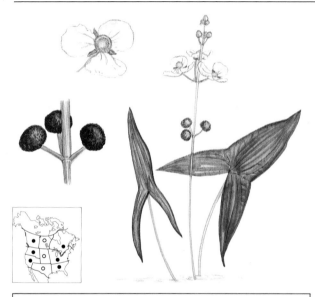

Flowers borne in whorls of three, along leafless flower stalks emerging from the water. Each flower has three white petals. Fruits borne in globular clusters.

An erect plant, up to 3ft. tall, with a clump of distinctive leaves emerging out of the water. Each leaf has a long stalk and a broad arrow-shaped blade, and exudes milky juice if damaged.

Found in water at the margins of ponds and streams, in marshes and ditches throughout southern Canada and the USA but less common in the far north and south.

There are several similar widespread species of Arrowheads in North America; this is one of the most common. The related Water Plantains have branched flower stalks and ovate leaves emerging from the water.

Flowering period: July–October.

:⁊ WATER LILY

Flowers floating, 3–5in. across, growing on long stalks from stems buried in the mud. Each has many white or pink scented petals, smaller in the center. Fruits like berries, ripen under water and release floating seeds.

A perennial aquatic plant with large creeping stems buried in the mud at the bottom of the water. The round leaves are borne on long stalks so that they float on the surface. They grow up to 12in. across and are purple beneath.

Found in lakes, ponds and slow-moving streams in much of the USA and southern Canada but more common in the east and generally absent west of the Rockies.

This is one of two common Water Lily species found in N. America — the other is similar but has no scent. The **Yellow Water Lily** has ovate floating leaves and yellow floating flowers. Floating Hearts have much smaller floating leaves and umbels of white flowers.

Flowering period: June–September.

Other Common Species

Moss Phlox (1) Prostrate stems form dense cushion with small leaves & wheel-shaped flowers in spring. Prairies & stony ground in C & W USA & Can.

Early Saxifrage (2) Rosettes of ovate hairy leaves & erect, sticky flowering stalks with clusters of flowers. Woods & rocks in E USA & Can.

Wintergreen (3) Long-stalked hairless, ovate leaves form rosette. Nodding flowers on erect stems have 5 petals. Moist woods throughout.

White Camas (4) From bulb grows erect stem with linear, sheathing leaves near base & spike of flowers. Woods & meadows scattered throughout.

Wild Sarsaparilla (5) Underground stem produces one large leaf & a flowering stem with umbels of flowers. Woods in C & E USA & in Can.

Other Common Species

Whitlow Grass (1) Small annual rosette-forming weed with a few tiny flowers on branched erect stems. Smooth broad pods. Roadsides & lawns.

Locoweed (2) Clump of silky stems & pinnate leaves with sprays of pea-like flowers on long stalks in axils. Damp meadows. C & W USA & S Can.

Pussytoes (3) Mats of rosettes with woolly connecting stems & leaves. Flowers with papery bracts in terminal heads. Dry grassland & woods throughout.

Jimsonweed (4) Coarse erect plant with large toothed leaves. White or mauve funnel-shaped flowers in axils. Waste places throughout.

Dutchman's Breeches (5) Lacy blue-green leaves & flowering stems with sprays of waxen flowers, like pantaloons. Woods, E & NC USA & Can.

Other Common Species

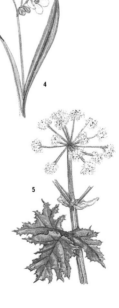

Indian Chickweed (1)
Prostrate stems bear whorls of
leaves & flowers with white-
margined sepals & no petals.
Waste places & fields
throughout.

Cryptantha (2) Small hairy
plant with erect stems, simple
leaves and dense terminal
spikes of tubular flowers. Dry
sandy places in SC & W USA.

Milkwort (3) Small erect plant
with leaves in whorls & spikes
of tubular flowers, each with 2
'wing' sepals. Dry woods,
grassy places. E & C USA &
Can.

Spring Beauty (4) Corm with
a few basal leaves & erect stem
with 2 leaves & terminal
cluster of flowers. Moist
woods. E USA & Can.

Cow Parsnip (5) Very large,
erect woolly plant with rank
smell. Flower umbels up to
8in. across, often purplish.
Roadsides, meadows
throughout.

Flower heads are bright yellow with ray florets only and no central disk; they are borne singly on leafless stalks. Flowers followed by distinctive "clocks", round balls of seeds, each with a parachute of hairs.

A small rosette-forming perennial plant with a long thin taproot and a clump of deep green entire or sinuate leaves. Flower stems are hollow and they, and the leaves, exude white "milk" when broken, which stains the fingers.

A familiar weed in lawns, gardens, roadsides and waste ground throughout the USA and southern Canada. European alien.

There are many members of the daisy family with similar flowers. They have ray florets only and many species have basal rosettes of leaves. They include the Goatsbeards, Hawk's-beards, Hawkweeds and **Sowthistles**; some have solitary flowers, in others the flowers are in clusters.

Flowering period: March–September. (P) All year.

Golden Butterweed (1)

Flower heads formed only of yellow tubular florets, almost enclosed in a "cup" of green bracts; borne in small clusters in the axils of the upper leaves. Seeds spindle-shaped, with many long white hairs and blow freely in the wind.

A small annual weed with a branched stem, up to one foot tall. Leaves are irregularly toothed, may be cottony and the upper ones have clasping bases; they are alternately arranged.

Found in waste places, on roadsides and as a weed of cultivated ground throughout the USA and Canada. European alien.

The related native Butterweeds and Ragworts may have similar flower heads to Groundsel or may have ray florets around the outside of the head. Many grow in wet meadows and woods. Golden Butterweed (inset) has heart-shaped leaves and grows in wet meadows and woods in eastern USA and Canada.

Flowering period: Throughout most of the year.

Common Cinquefoil (1), Rough Cinquefoil (2)

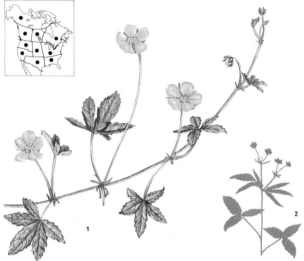

Flowers solitary or borne in branched clusters on long flower stalks in the leaf axils; yellow or rarely white with five petals alternating with the sepals, like small single roses. Fruits borne in clusters in persistent sepals.

Hairy perennial creeping plants, rooting at the nodes or clump-forming plants, all with alternate, compound leaves. Leaves are palmately divided into five sections, or pinnate, or three-lobed, often long-stalked, with toothed leaflets.

Found on prairies and in fields, in woods, on roadsides and waste ground, in dry or damp places throughout N. America. Several are European aliens.

There are many common Cinquefoils, especially in the prairie regions. Common Cinquefoil grows in fields and dry woods. Silverweed has pinnate leaves with white-silky hairs beneath; Rough Cinquefoil, the most widespread, has only three leaflets on its leaves.

Flowering period: May–October.

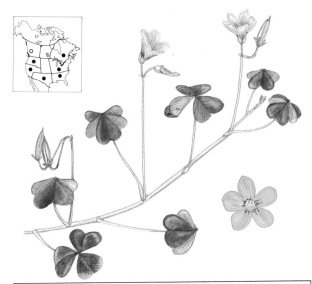

Flowers borne singly or in pairs at the ends of long flower stalks, growing from the axils of the leaves. Each has five yellow petals. Fruits are cylindrical capsules.

A small weed with prostrate stems and tufts of leaves and roots growing at the nodes. Leaves like long-stalked, heart-shaped clover leaves, with three leaflets which all fold down at night. One form has purple leaves.

Persistent weeds in lawns and flower beds, as well as on roadsides and waste ground, throughout southern Canada and the USA except the north central states.

Several other Yellow Wood-sorrels are found in N. America. All have similar leaves, but some are not creeping species and in others the flowers are borne in clusters. The folding of the leaves distinguishes them from **Cinquefoils** and the flowers from **Clovers**.

Flowering period: March–November.

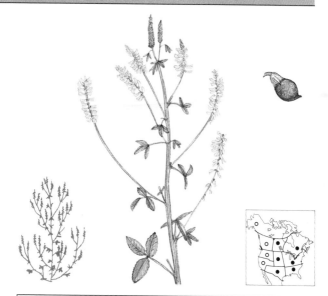

Flowers many, like yellow pea flowers, and smelling of new-mown hay; borne in loose spikes on long flower stalks in the leaf axils. Pods egg-shaped with transverse ridges and brown when ripe.

A much branched, more or less erect biennial plant, usually about 3ft. tall. The compound leaves each have three leaflets and a stipule clasping the base of the leaf stalk.

Found on roadsides, in fields and waste places throughout the USA and much of Canada, but commoner in the east and midwest than in the Pacific states.

White Sweet Clover is very similar and also common, more common than Yellow Sweet Clover in the Pacific states. It can be recognized by its white flowers. Both are European aliens. The related yellow-flowered **Locoweeds** have pinnate leaves while yellow-flowered **Lupines** have palmate leaves.

Flowering period: April–October.

Pea-like flowers yellow or streaked with red, borne in clusters of up to eight flowers on long stalks in the leaf axils. The cluster of pods which follows resembles a bird's foot. Pods twist as they open.

A small, mat-forming, somewhat hairy, perennial plant with many thin branching stems clothed with compound leaves. Each leaf has five leaflets, two of which are situated at the base of the leaf stalk.

Found in dry grassland, roadsides and waste places throughout the USA and southern Canada. European alien.

There are many small mat-forming plants with yellow flowers belonging to the pea family, including the Medicks and Hop Clovers but their flowers are usually smaller and are often borne in distinct heads. Hill Lotus is a gray-hairy Calif. species with solitary flowers.

Flowering period: May–September.

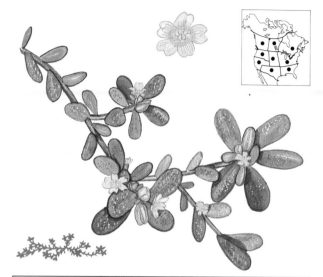

Flowers borne singly, in the center of the terminal leaf rosettes, only opening in the sun. Petals four to six, usually five, pale yellow and soon falling. Fruits are egg-shaped capsules.

An annual weed with many succulent prostrate branches, up to 2ft. long. Leaves opposite, shining and fleshy, paddle-shaped, the terminal ones borne in rosettes.

Found in waste places and fields and also grows as a garden weed throughout the USA and southern Canada. European alien.

None of the other Purslanes are common or widespread. Some of the **Stonecrops** are prostrate and succulent and can be distinguished from Purslane by their leaves which are alternate or grow in whorls and by their starry flowers which are borne in terminal clusters on erect stems.

Flowering period: May–October.

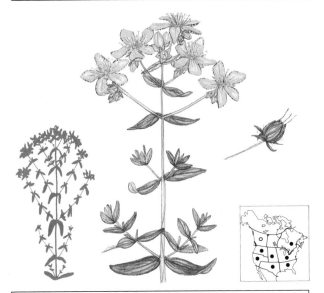

Flowers numerous, borne in branched clusters at the tops of the stems. Each has five yellow petals with black dots on the margins and, like other St John's Worts, many yellow stamens at the center.

A hairless, branched perennial plant, up to 2ft. tall, spreading by leafy offshoots. The stems bear many opposite, stalkless ovate leaves, marked with translucent dots.

Roadsides, fields and waste places and a persistent spreading weed in some places. Throughout much of the USA and southern Canada. European alien.

One of many St John's Worts, several of which are grown in gardens. Many of the species grow in wet places where they may be confused with **Yellow Loosestrife** but St John's Worts can be recognized by their distinctively numerous yellow stamens.

Flowering period: June–September.

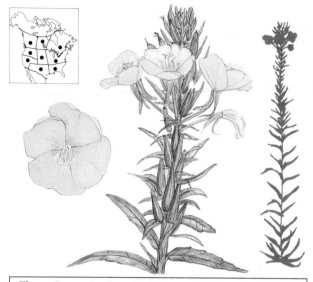

Flowers large and yellow with four petals and a cross-shaped stigma in the center; borne in a dense terminal spike and opening a few at a time in the late afternoon. Cylindrical capsules grow at an angle.

A biennial plant which forms a rosette of basal leaves in the first year and a tall flowering spike in the second, up to 5ft. tall, with many lance-shaped, spirally arranged leaves.

Found in waste places, in fields and on roadsides throughout the USA and southern Canada, but more common in central and eastern areas.

There are many Evening Primroses, varying from rosette-forming mountain and desert species to larger more erect plants of roadsides and prairies. Their flowers open in the late afternoon. Most have yellow, a few have white flowers. The related Suncups have flowers which only open in sun.

Flowering period: June–October.

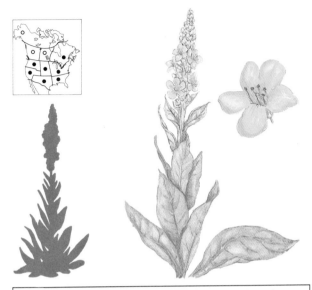

Flowers yellow with five petals, crowded together and opening a few at a time on the very large woolly flower spike. Fruits are woolly capsules.

A biennial plant with a rosette of large woolly leaves in the first year and a tall, erect flowering stem in the second, up to 6ft. tall. This has many white woolly leaves with characteristic bases running down the stem.

Found on roadsides, in waste places and in fields throughout the USA and southern Canada. European alien.

There are three other common Mulleins, two others are not white woolly and appear green, although they are hairy. The third is woolly but its leaf bases do not run down the stem. They all have similar flower spikes and yellow, or occasionally white, flowers.

Flowering period: June–September.

47

Common (1), Creeping (2)

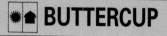

Flowers bowl-shaped, with five bright yellow, overlapping petals, shiny on the inside; borne on long, upright, branching stalks. Cluster of green beaked fruits, each containing a single seed.

Upright or creeping perennial plants, up to 3ft. high, with basal clumps of long-stalked, deeply divided leaves and erect, branched stems bearing a few similar leaves with flowers on long stems in the leaf axils. All have acrid sap.

Found in grassy places throughout much of N. America except the desert areas of the south and the extreme north. Some of the most common are European aliens.

Common species include Common Buttercup which has sepals pressed against the petals; Bulbous Buttercup in which the sepals are reflexed; Creeping Buttercup which has creeping stems, rooting at the nodes; and Bristly Buttercup with hairy stems.

Flowering period: May–September.

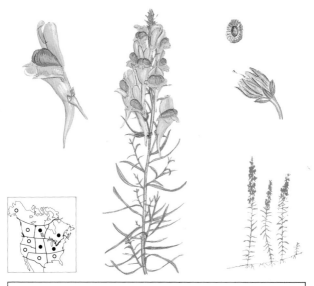

Flowers like snapdragons, bright yellow with orange palates and long straight spurs, borne in dense leafy spikes at the tops of the flowering stems. Fruits are five-lobed capsules cupped in the persistent calyx.

A perennial plant with creeping underground stems, from which spring many erect, hairless flowering stems, up to 3ft. tall, clothed with many linear, bright green leaves.

Found on roadsides and dry places including waste ground, throughout the USA and Canada, but only occasionally in the Pacific states. European alien.

Dalmatian Toadflax, which is found in central USA and southern Canada, is similar but the yellow flowers do not have orange palates and its leaves are oval.

Flowering period: June–October.

Conspicuous flowers borne singly on long stems; each has 10–20 large, bright yellow ray florets and a brown or purplish, cone-shaped disk. Seeds dark in color with no hairs.

An annual or perennial plant with a basal clump of more or less lance-shaped leaves and one or several flowering stems, with a few leaves, up to 3ft. tall. Stems and leaves are all covered with bristly hairs.

Found on roadsides, on the prairies especially in disturbed areas, in fields and meadows throughout the USA and southern Canada.

This is one of the commonest of the flowers known as Coneflowers. Green-centered Coneflower, another common species, has a green disk and deeply divided leaves. The similar Sneezeweeds and Tickseeds can be identified by the three- or four-lobed tips to their ray florets.

Flowering period: May–July. (P) June–August.

COMMON SUNFLOWER ☀🏠

Wild plants have many flower heads, about one inch across, with yellow ray florets and central reddish disks. Escaped cultivated forms have far fewer, much larger flower heads. Fruits white with black streaks, containing edible seeds.

Wild native plants are branched annuals, up to 10ft. tall, with large, rather pointed heart-shaped, dark green leaves, borne alternately on slender stalks. The whole plant is rough to the touch.

Found on roadsides and in grasslands, especially on the prairies, but also throughout the USA and southern Canada.

One of many yellow-flowered composites including other Sunflowers, Tickseeds, Coneflowers (see **Black-eyed Susan**), Mule-ears etc. which differ in size, in the color and form of the central flower disk, in the angle of the ray florets and in the form of their leaves.

Flowering period: July–October. (P) February–October.

Flowers yellow and distinctive in shape, like hooded, spurred tubes with four petals, "balanced on their stalks"; borne in small sprays growing in the leaf axils of the topmost leaves. Fruits are cylindrical capsules.

An annual or biennial plant forming an untidy clump of weak sprawling stems with smooth, pale blue-green, deeply dissected leaves. The plant is brittle with watery sap.

Found in open sandy or stony places, in open woods and along roads and railways throughout southern Canada and the USA except the southeast.

There are several other yellow Corydalis species in N. America but only one, Yellow Corydalis, is at all common and its petals are frilled at the open end of the flower. Pale Corydalis has pink flowers with yellow tips and the related Fumitory also has pink flowers tipped with purple.

Flowering period: May–July.

CALIFORNIA POPPY ☀

Brilliant bowl-shaped, yellow or orange flowers have four petals and a large four-lobed stigma; borne on long stems, with circular double-rimmed "toruses" on which the flowers sit. Fruits are long capsules, opening by two valves.

A very variable smooth, annual or perennial plant, up to 2ft. tall, which forms a spreading clump of long-stalked, blue-green, lacy leaves and weak flowering stems with many similar leaves. The plant has clear watery sap.

Found in open and grassy places in southern and southwestern USA from the coast to desert areas.

Californian Poppies can be distinguished from other members of the poppy family by the four-lobed stigma, the two-valved capsule and the clear sap. Many Poppies have colored sap. True Poppies have very distinctive capsules, like peppershakers with holes beneath the rim at the top.

Flowering period: February–September.

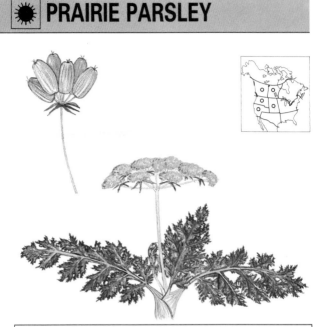

Flowers yellow and tiny, borne in dense compound umbels terminating the erect flower stalks. Beneath each small umbel are several long bracts. The large seeds are borne in pairs on erect stalks, each one is flattened and winged.

A perennial plant with a short stem and alternate, finely divided, more or less hairy, blue-gray leaves with distinctive sheathing stalks, and erect flowering stems, up to 18in. tall, bearing umbels of flowers.

Found on dry open ground and bare slopes on the prairies of the USA and Canada and the Pacific states and B.C.

This is one of many similar species found in western areas in open dry places, but most are local and few are widespread. Other yellow-flowered members of the carrot family include Wild Parsnip which grows on roadsides and waste places throughout N. America, Parsley, Dill and Fennel.

Flowering period: April–June.

WALLFLOWER ☀

Flowers borne in erect spikes which lengthen as they age. Petals four, varying from yellow to orange or brown. Fruits are long pods, up to 4in. long, square in cross section, borne more or less upright.

An erect biennial plant, with a clump of lance-shaped leaves in the first year and flowering stems in the second, up to 3ft. tall. Leaves on flowering stems are linear, grayish and arranged alternately.

Found in dry stony places and prairies, mostly in western and central USA and Canada and rare in the east.

There are many other Wallflower species in western USA, differing mainly in the form of their seed pods and in the shape of their leaves. Wormseed is a similar European species naturalized throughout, with much smaller flowers and fruits (only 1–2in. long.)

Flowering period: (midwest) May–June. (P) March–July.

Blazing Star (1)

Flowers with five yellow petals and many stamens; borne in small clusters or singly in the axils of the upper leaves. Fruit forms below the flower and is an elongated capsule, opening at the top.

An annual plant with erect, shining white stems, up to 18in. tall. The lobed, stalkless leaves are alternate, rough to the touch and cling to clothing, becoming brittle when old.

Found in dry sandy places in central and western USA and west of the Rockies in Canada.

The Stickleafs and Blazing Stars are related species found in dry areas of central and western USA. They are generally similar but Blazing Stars have much larger flowers. The Blazing Star illustrated has stamens which resemble petals; it is one of the most widespread species.

Flowering period: March–July.

Plains Prickly Pear

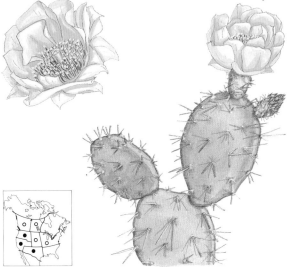

Flowers are usually large and solitary, with many similar yellow petals and many yellow or orange stamens. Fruits are spiny berries which form beneath the flowers.

These cactuses have flattened, jointed stems, with no ribs. Two kinds of spines are present in the tufts, long central spines and tiny bristles around them. Small fleshy leaves are soon shed. Most common species form spreading mats.

Found on dry prairies, plains and desert areas, mainly in western and central areas of the USA but a few species are found in Canada and in the east.

The Plains Prickly Pear is the most widely distributed, together with the Pygmy Prickly Pear, a similar but much smaller species also found in the east. The most common eastern Prickly Pear has bristles, together with only an occasional spine. There are many western desert species.

Flowering period: (S) May–June. (N) July–August.

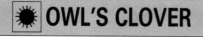

Flowers yellow, tubular and two-lipped; borne close together in narrow spikes terminating the stems. The spikes contain many green leafy bracts as well as flowers. Fruits are small flattened capsules.

A small annual plant, up to 18in. tall, with a few erect stems covered with soft hairs. The lower parts of the stems bear alternate, narrow, softly hairy leaves while the upper parts bear the flowers.

Found on dry prairies and in sagebrush scrub across the prairie states of the USA and in central southern Canada and also in the west.

There are several other Owl's Clovers in western N. America but this is the most widespread. They vary in flower color from yellow to purple, in the color of the bracts and in the shape of the stem leaves. The related **Indian Paintbrushes** have more brightly colored bracts in the flower spikes.

Flowering period: June–August.

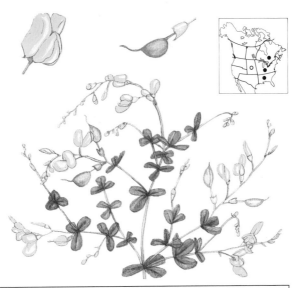

Flowers yellow and pea-like, borne in loose flower spikes at the tops of the stems, numerous. Pods smooth and rounded, with a persistent toothed calyx.

A bushy perennial plant, up to 3ft. tall, with hairless stems and many, more or less stalkless, grayish-green clover-like leaves, each with three leaflets. The plant blackens when dried.

Found in open woodland and clearings in eastern areas of the USA and in southeastern Canada.

May be distinguished from **Milkvetches** by the clover-like leaves, from **Clovers** by the loose flower spikes and from **Sweet Clovers** by the absence of the scent of new-mown hay. This species may be distinguished from other Indigos by its blackened appearance when dry.

Flowering period: April–August.

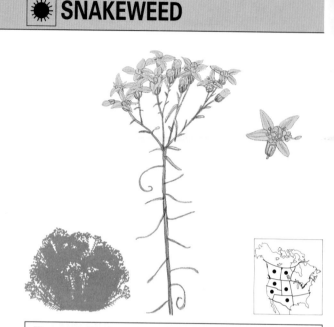

Flowers small and numerous with yellow ray florets and central disk florets; borne in terminal, flat-topped clusters at the tops of the stems. Flowers followed by scaly seeds.

An untidy, clump-forming, sub-shrubby perennial plant with many brittle, slender stems, more or less erect and growing up to 18in. tall. The alternately arranged leaves are thread-like and hairy.

Found in dry prairies and sagebrush scrub in western and central areas of the USA and Canada, especially in land that has been overgrazed.

There are a few **Goldenrods** that grow in dry prairies but they have broader leaves and hairy seeds. Rabbit Brush is a much grayer plant and its flowers have no ray florets; while Colorado Rubber Weed is a dwarf, cushion-like plant and its larger flowers have a few broad ray florets.

Flowering period: July–September.

GOLDENRODS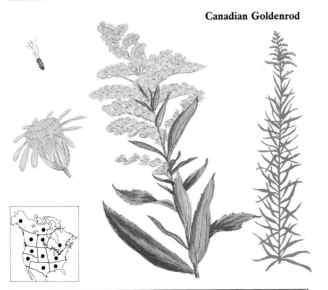

Canadian Goldenrod

Flower heads tiny, with yellow ray florets and central yellow disks; borne in distinctive spray-like plumes, flat-topped clusters or spikes at the tops of the upright stems. The many seeds have feathery white or brownish hairs.

Perennial plants with many upright, straight, leafy stems growing from horizontally creeping stems, so that a clump or wide colony may result. Leaves alternate, simple, with smooth or toothed margins.

Found in many habitats from open woods and dry open ground to rich woods and marshes, roadsides, prairies etc. throughout N. America except the far north.

Amongst the most common are Canadian Goldenrod, Late Goldenrod which grows up to 7ft. tall, Showy Goldenrod with large leaves and tighter, less plume-like clusters of flowers and Missouri Goldenrod with flat-topped flower clusters.

Flowering period: July–October.

Pink Monkeyflower (1)

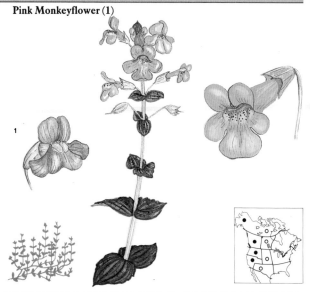

Flowers solitary on long stalks, growing in the leaf axils of the uppermost leaves; tubular and two-lipped with a large open lower lip. The throat is closed by hairy ridges and may be red-spotted. Fruit a capsule enclosed by calyx.

A perennial, somewhat succulent, plant, up to 3ft. tall, with creeping, rooting stems and erect flower-bearing stems growing from them. All stems are leafy, with opposite, toothed, hairless leaves.

Found in wet places and beside streams in northern central and western areas of the USA, but not in the south or east, and in southern Canada.

There are many Monkeyflowers in N. America with yellow, red or pink flowers. Pink Monkeyflower (inset), is an eastern species. Most are found in the west, especially in Calif. Monkeyflowers can be distinguished from **Beardstongues** by the presence of the ridges in the throats of their flowers.

Flowering period: March–August.

YELLOW LADY'S SLIPPER

Showy Lady's Slipper (1)

One or two large, showy flowers are produced. Each has four long twisted, greenish-yellow 'petals' streaked with purple, and a conspicuous yellow, pouched lip. Fruit is a brown capsule.

A perennial plant with an underground stem, from which is produced each year a single flowering stem with three or four large ovate leaves. These are up to 8in. long and have pointed tips and prominent ribs.

Found in rich moist woods and mossy bogs throughout southern Canada and most of the USA except Calif.; in mountain areas in the south where it is much rarer.

There are other Lady's Slippers found in N. America; all have similar shaped flowers but some are white and pink. The most common of these are the Showy Lady's Slipper (inset) and the Moccasin Flower. Several yellow or brown-flowered species grow in Californian woods.

Flowering period: April–July.

Other Common Species

Lousewort (1) Basal rosettes of soft-hairy, pinnate leaves & erect stem with dense spike of hooded flowers. Moist open woods in C & E USA & Can.

Yellow Water Lily (2) Bowl-shaped flowers have 5–7 fleshy yellow sepals. Flask-like fruit ripens above water. Ponds & lakes in N USA & Can.

Fringed Loosestrife (3) Erect stems with opposite ovate leaves and whorls of tubular flowers. Throughout, except SC USA & N Can. Moist woods.

Beggarticks (4) Branched stems have terminal clusters of dull yellow flower heads, cupped in long bracts. Damp woods, waste places & meadows throughout.

Sowthistle (5) Erect stem with milky sap and alternate spiky-toothed leaves. Flower heads in terminal clusters. Roadsides and waste places throughout.

Stonecrop (1) Mat-forming plant with fleshy leaves & starry flowers on erect stems. Roadsides & rocks in N & E USA & S Can.

Ground Cherry (2) Sticky stems have large leaves and solitary flowers in leaf axils. Fruits like lanterns. Waste places & roadsides, E & C areas.

White Mustard (3) Flowers with 4 petals in loose terminal spikes. Fruits are beaded, hairy pods with long beaks. Waste places throughout.

Prince's Plume (4) Flowers have 4 petals, each with a long basal claw and a broader blade; borne in dense plume. Prairies in C & W USA.

Wild Yellow Lily (5) Tall erect plant with whorls of leaves, growing from a bulb. Several flowers nod at top of stem. Meadows E & W USA & Can.

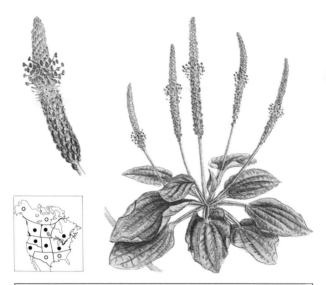

Flowers borne in spikes usually about 12in. long, appearing to be green since the whitish petals are so small. Anthers conspicuous, at first mauve, later yellowish. Fruiting spike similar in shape, but brown with many small, hard fruits.

A perennial rosette-forming plant with many broad, rounded, almost hairless, long-stalked leaves, each up to 8in. long. These leaves have well defined veins.

A very common weed, throughout the USA and Canada, especially on bare trodden ground in waste places, back yards, roadsides and tracks. European alien.

One of several common Plantains differing mainly in the shape of their leaves and flower spikes. Another very common species is English Plantain with long and narrow, upright leaves and short fat flower spikes with conspicuous white anthers, terminating long stems.

Flowering period: April–frost.

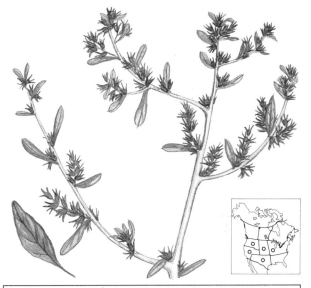

Flowers green, with five sepals and no petals, borne in crowded clusters in the leaf axils, each with three sharp bracts below. Fruits are bladder-like, each with one seed. Dead dried plant tumbles with the wind.

A hairless, annual plant with many branched stems forming a prostrate mat. Stems white or purplish, covered with many small, lance-shaped, alternately arranged leaves.

Found in waste places and cultivated fields in central and western areas of the USA.

Several other related species (Amaranths) are weeds of farms and waste ground, including the Pigweeds which are erect branching plants with spikes of axillary flowers. Russian Tumbleweed is the familiar ball-like tumbleweed of western desert areas.

Flowering period: July–frost.

Curly Dock (1), Whorled Dock (2)

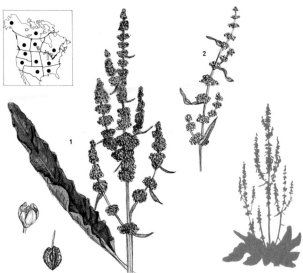

Flowers greenish-brown in color and borne in whorls on large, upright, branching spikes. Fruits are more colorful than flowers, three-sided in shape, often with three unequal red swellings in the angles.

Large perennial weeds, up to 4ft. high, with a long tap root and a clump of large, long-stalked leaves, varying in their shape and in their edges depending on species. A traditional remedy for nettle stings.

Found in waste places, on cultivated ground, in fields and grassy places throughout the USA and Canada. Some of the commonest are European aliens.

Common species include Curly Dock with long leaves with distinctive curly edges; Broad Dock with wavy, not curly edges to the leaves; and Whorled Dock in which the flowers are borne in widely separated whorls within the flower spike. Sorrels are also closely related to docks.

Flowering period: Summer, followed by fruits in fall.

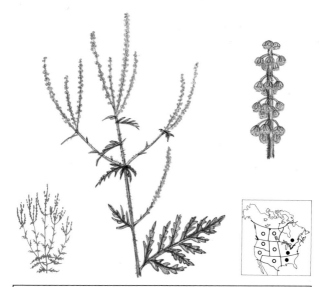

Flower heads numerous; male heads nodding, borne in long flower spikes at the tops of the branches, producing clouds of pollen. Female heads borne in tight clusters in upper leaf axils.

An annual weed with a branched, leafy stem, up to 5ft. tall; stem four-angled and hairy. Leaves deeply divided, lowermost opposite but uppermost alternate, green on upper surface but gray-hairy beneath.

Found on roadsides, in waste places and fields throughout the USA and southern Canada but introduced and not as common in northern central and western parts of this area.

Giant Ragweed has similar flowers but is about twice as large and has three-lobed leaves. Western Ragweed is a spreading, perennial plant, more common in the west than in the east, with hairy divided leaves. The similar Mugworts have leafy flower spikes and all the flowers are the same.

Flowering period: August–frost, causes hay-fever.

Flowers small and petal-less, borne in green 'tassels' in the axils of the leaves, male and female flowers on separate plants. Fruits are small seed-like nutlets enclosed in the persistent calyx.

A large perennial plant, with a clump of upright four-angled stems, 2–3ft. high, bearing pairs of roughly toothed, deep green, pointed leaves. The whole plant is clothed with stinging hairs.

Found in woods, waste places and on cultivated land and roadsides in eastern and central USA and in most of Canada, except the far north. European alien.

May be mistaken for Hedge-nettles and Dead-nettles (including **Henbit**) which have no stinging hairs but do have large, hooded flowers. The similar Slender Nettle has fewer stinging hairs and narrower, more pointed leaves.

Flowering period: April–October.

Flowers small and green with five green petals, borne in dense leafy spikes made up of many smaller flower clusters. Seeds brown and enclosed in persistent petals.

A large annual weed, up to 2ft. tall, with reddish, mealy stems (covered with bladder-like hairs) and large leaves. Leaves toothed, lowermost broad and rhomboidal, uppermost lance-shaped, deep green above and mealy beneath.

Found in waste places, on roadsides and cultivated ground, particularly where soil is rich in nitrogen, throughout the USA and Canada. European alien.

One of many common and widespread Goosefoots and Oraches not easy to distinguish from each other. They differ in odor, leaf shape, hairiness and flower structure but the differences are not always easy to spot except to the expert.

Flowering period: June–frost.

71

Cypress Spurge (1)

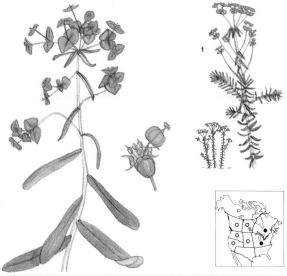

Only some of the erect stems bear flowers. These are green, tiny, borne in umbels and cupped in yellow-green, leafy bracts that are often mistaken for the petals. Fruits are warty capsules.

A perennial plant, spreading by creeping underground roots, from which grow many erect leafy stems, up to 2ft. tall. The plant is hairless and contains acrid milky juice. Leaves are alternate, linear and stalkless.

Found on roadsides and waste places, especially in river flats, throughout southern Canada and much of the USA but not in the south. European alien.

There are many Spurges in N. America, some of them common. Some, like Leafy and Cypress Spurges (inset), are spreading plants with many leafy shoots; others, like Wartweed, are annual weeds with a single shoot and a terminal umbel of typical green spurge flowers.

Flowering period: May–August.

Flowers widely separated in long, erect spikes, carried obliquely on short stalks; green calyx more or less vase-shaped, partly enclosing five spoon-shaped purple petals. Fruits are beaked capsules, enclosed in calyx.

A perennial plant with a rosette of long-stalked leaves with tough leathery, rounded, scallop-shaped leaf blades. The leaf stalks are hairy. Flowers are borne on erect, leafless flower stalks, up to 2ft. tall.

Found in prairie grassland and foothill areas and in open woodland in northern USA and throughout Canada except the extreme eastern areas.

There are many species of Alumroots found throughout N. America, varying in flower color from pink to white and green. Many are woodland species. They are related to the similar Miterworts but these plants can be immediately recognized by their fringed petals.

Flowering period: June–July.

Corn Speedwell (1), Brooklime (2)

Flowers blue or white, borne singly or in sprays in the leaf axils. Each flower is tubular with four petals, one on each side, one at the top and one at the bottom. Fruits are capsules, cupped in persistent sepals.

Erect or prostrate, annual or perennial plants forming a dense mat or clump of stems with opposite, simple, often toothed leaves. They may be hairless or covered with fine hairs. Many are weeds while some are garden species.

Found in a variety of habitats from waste places and roadsides, to lawns and meadows. There are also several aquatic species. Throughout the USA and Canada.

Several weedy species, like the annual Corn Speedwell, Thyme-leaved Speedwell with solitary flowers and Common Speedwell with sprays of flowers are found in waste places and on roadsides. Brooklime is a succulent plant found growing on the edges of stream banks.

Flowering period: May–September.

Flowers pale blue, with five petals joined together only at the base and slightly overlapping; borne in small, very loose clusters at the tops of all the branches of the stems. Fruits are capsules.

A smooth annual plant, 2–3ft. tall, with several slender, erect, loosely branched stems growing from one crown. The narrow leaves are well separated from each other and borne alternately. This is the cultivated species of flax.

Found on roadsides, in waste places and old fields where it has escaped from cultivation throughout the USA and Canada. Introduced from Europe.

Wild Flaxes may have blue, pink or yellow flowers. Many are delicate plants similar in form to the Cultivated Flax but others are more leafy. They usually have stems which are repeatedly forked so that the two new stems diverge equally from the original.

Flowering period: Throughout spring and summer.

American Vetch (1), Tufted Vetch (2)

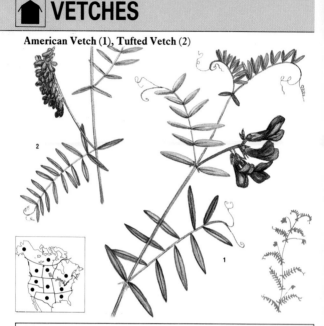

Flowers pea-like but with the wings attached to the keel, red-purple or blue-purple in color; borne in small clusters or on long sprays in the leaf axils. Pods flattened from side to side, opening by two valves.

Small annual to perennial twining plants, with thin vine-like stems and tendrils on the leaves. Leaves alternate, pinnate, usually with 6–20 opposite leaflets and with the simple or branched tendril at the end.

Found on roadsides, in waste places and fields as well as in grassy places and woodland throughout the USA and Canada. Some of the commonest are European aliens.

Several of the Vetches are widespread and common, including the American Vetch with 4–9 reddish-purple flowers in each spray; Spring Vetch with 1–2 similar flowers in each leaf axil; Tufted Vetch with many blue flowers in one-sided sprays.

Flowering period: May–July.

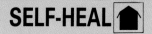

Flowers purplish-blue, tubular and two-lipped, the upper lip arched over and the lower lip three-lobed; borne in dense terminal spikes containing hairy bracts. Calyxes also hairy. Fruit consists of four ridged nutlets.

A small, hairy, perennial plant, up to 12in. tall forming a clump of four-angled, leafy stems that lie on the ground and then turn upwards to bear flower spikes. The deep green, opposite leaves are simple and ovate.

Found on roadsides and lawns, in fields and meadows throughout the USA and Canada. European alien.

Bugle is a related species but can be easily distinguished from Self-heal for it is a smooth, hairless plant and its leaves are often bronzed. The flowers of **Skullcaps** are borne in loose spikes or singly in the leaf axils.

Flowering period: April–September.

☀ HAREBELL

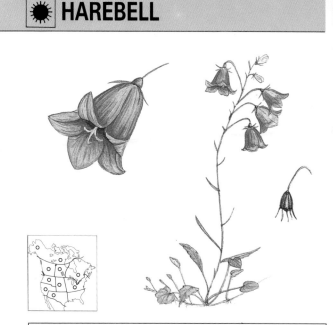

Usually a few blue, bell-shaped flowers nodding on the delicate stems on long stalks; buds erect. The sepals are very narrow. Fruit a rounded capsule with five sections, opening by pores at the base to release the seeds.

A delicate little perennial plant, usually about 6in. tall, with a clump of heart-shaped basal leaves. From this grow several erect, slender wiry stems with alternately arranged, dark green, linear leaves.

Grassy places and meadows, especially in mountain areas. Throughout much of Canada and the USA except the far north and the southeast.

There are nearly 30 Bellflowers in N. America but none are particularly common or widespread. The Harebell is the most likely to be seen but others include Bedstraw Bellflower and Marsh Bellflower, both of which grow in wet areas. They have pale blue, more erect flowers with broader sepals.

Flowering period: June–September.

PRAIRIE ANEMONE ☀

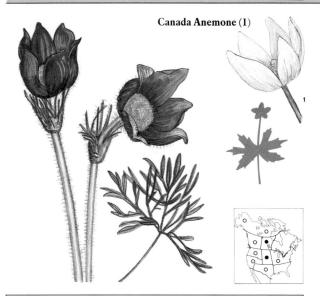

Canada Anemone (1)

Flowers borne singly on separate stalks, cupped in leafy bracts; each has five to seven blue-violet or white petal-like sepals, many stamens and a central "seed" boss. Seed-heads distinctive, each seed with a feathery plume.

A perennial plant forming a clump of silky, long-stalked, divided leaves which appear after the flowers, when the plant is in seed. Each leaf is divided into three sections, and then subdivided again.

Found in prairie grassland and open woodland throughout the prairie states and provinces of the USA and Canada.

There are several other common Anemones. Canada Anemones (inset) are similar to Prairie Anemones but have white flowers; Windflowers have clumps of divided leaves and white to purple flowers borne above the clump. Thimbleweeds have similar flowers but long woolly seed-heads.

Flowering period: April–May.

☀ **DELPHINIUMS** OR **LARKSPURS**

Dwarf Larkspur (1), Bilobed Larkspur (2)

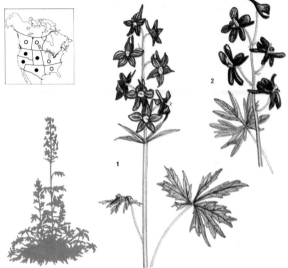

Flowers usually blue-violet, sometimes white or bi-colored. Both sepals and petals are colored and the flowers are distinctively shaped, with a long spur at the back formed by both sepals and petals. Fruits are clusters of pods.

Mostly perennial plants, up to 3ft. tall, forming a clump of long-stalked, palmately divided leaves and several erect stems bearing smaller leaves and a terminal spike of flowers. These plants are poisonous.

There are several widespread prairie species and many different delphiniums in the Pacific states, especially in Calif. Garden varieties may escape onto roadsides in the east.

Dwarf Larkspur is an eastern woodland species, while Bilobed Larkspur is found in western and central USA, especially in the prairies. The most widespread prairie species has white flowers. In Calif. Larkspurs grow in coastal areas, in woods and forests and in the chaparral as well as in grassy areas.

Flowering period: March–May.

80

Wild Lupine (1), Blue-pod Lupine (2)

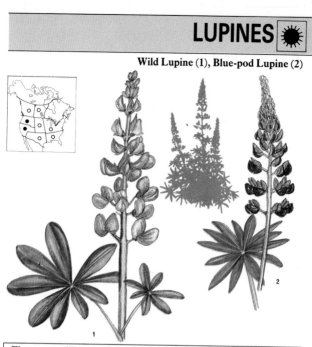

Flowers pea-like, blue in most species, but may be white or yellow, borne in spikes on tall erect flower stalks growing above the clump of leaves. Pods hairy or silky, up to 2in. long, flattened from side to side.

Erect biennial or perennial plants, usually about 2ft. tall, with a basal clump of long-stalked, palmately divided leaves having 7–15 leaflets. Some species are hairless, others densely hairy.

Found in open woodland, open dry ground, sagebrush scrub and on the Pacific coast. Many more species grow in western USA than in the east. A few are found in Canada.

The commonest of the eastern species is the Wild Lupine from which the garden forms are derived. Amongst the most common of the western forms are the Blue-pod Lupine which grows in moist woods and meadows; and Broadleaf Lupine which grows in mountain woods. Sulphur Lupine has yellow flowers.

Flowering period: April–May.

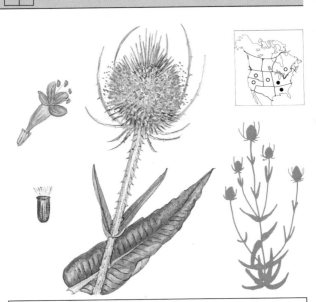

Blue-mauve flowers borne in distinctive, prickly flower heads, the earliest blooming in a ring around the center of the head and later flowers spreading up and down. Flower heads remain to form prickly fruits, the teasels.

A large biennial plant with a clump of prickly leaves in the first year. Erect, hollow, prickly stems grow up to 6ft. tall in the second year, bearing long lance-shaped, opposite leaves and flower heads.

Found in waste places, along roadsides and in meadows, especially where the land is wet, throughout much of N. America but rarer in the south and west. European alien.

Teasels belong to a family of their own but might be mistaken for Burdocks or **Thistles**. The ring of flowers is distinctive however; Burdocks and Thistles have flowers on top of a prickly receptacle and hairy seeds afterwards.

Flowers: July–Sept. Fruits: Sept.–Oct. and often persist.

SPIDERWORT

Flowers have three blue or purple petals; they are borne on long arching stalks in terminal clusters, on separate erect stems; each cluster is cupped in leafy bracts. Fruits are rounded capsules.

A perennial clump-forming plant formed of many long, brittle but soft, sword-like leaves, arching at the tips and up to 6ft. tall. The leaves have conspicuous sheathing bases.

Found in woods and on woodland edges, on roadsides and in prairies in eastern and northern central USA, usually in moist ground. Also grown in gardens.

There are several species of Spiderworts found in the USA and two more of them are relatively common in dry prairies, as well as the species described. They may have pink or blue flowers.

Flowering period: April–July.

Flowers blue or whitish, with a circle of ray florets and a central disk; borne in clusters on erect stalks in a spray at the top of the stem. Seeds have long hairs.

A biennial plant with a tall leafy stem, up to 4ft. tall. Leaves more or less lance-shaped, the lower ones deeply lobed or toothed, the uppermost stalkless. The plant is usually hairless or only slightly hairy.

Found in woods and meadows, and on woodland edges throughout Canada and the USA except the central southern area. Rarer in the west.

Three common Blue Lettuces are found in N. America. One is a perennial western species with large flowers in loose sprays; the others grow in the east. The related blue **Asters** have simple, untoothed leaves.

Flowering period: July–frost.

VIRGINIA BLUEBELL

Flowers funnel-shaped, pink in bud, turning blue as they open; borne in one-sided clusters at the tops of the erect stems. Fruits are four wrinkled nutlets, cupped in persistent sepals.

A smooth perennial plant, forming a clump of oval, long-stalked basal leaves, each up to 8in. long. The erect flowering stems grow up to 2ft. high and bear alternate, broad leaves and terminal flower clusters.

Found in moist rich woods in eastern USA and southeast Canada.

There are several very similar species found in southwestern USA and in the Pacific states, where they are known as Lungworts. Oysterleaf is a less common prostrate, mat-forming coastal relative found on northern coasts on both sides of the continent.

Flowering period: March–June.

85

:·: BLUE VERVAIN

Flower spikes resemble a candelabrum. Flowers open a few at a time, beginning at the base of each spike. Each bloom is tubular with five equal petal lobes, usually blue but may be pink or white. Fruit is four nutlets enclosed in calyx.

A roughly hairy, perennial plant with erect, branched, four-angled stems, 3–4ft. tall, the branches growing upwards and bearing opposite, lance-shaped, coarsely toothed leaves and dense terminal spikes of flowers.

Found in wet places, including fields and woods, roadsides and marshes throughout the USA and southern Canada.

There is another equally widespread species, with pinnately dissected leaves and obvious bracts in the flower spikes. Other Vervains have purple or violet flowers. Most are found in central and eastern areas of the USA.

Flowering period: June–October.

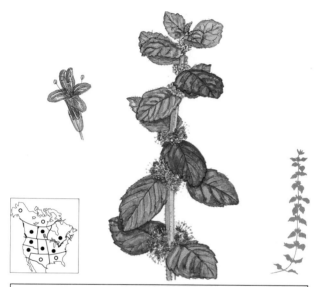

Flowers arranged in whorled clusters in the widely separated leaf axils of the upper leaves. Calyxes hairy, flowers tubular, lavender or pale pink. Fruits are small brown nutlets, in fours, in persistent calyxes.

A very variable perennial plant, up to 2ft. high, with many rather weak, four-angled stems. Often there are small hairs on the angles. Leaves ovate with toothed edges, opposite and aromatically scented.

Found in moist ground and wet places throughout the USA and most of Canada but absent from the far north and rare in southern USA.

There are several widespread Mints, including Peppermint, Spearmint and Apple Mint which can be recognized by their scents. These plants bear their flowers in dense spikes, not in widely separated whorls. Bugleweeds are scentless and have whorls of flowers in the leaf axils.

Flowering period: June–October.

Flowers blue-violet in color, with six petals, borne on leafless, branching flower stalks which grow directly from the base of the clump. Fruits are small round capsules.

A tufted, perennial, grass-like plant with a clump of linear, erect leaves, up to 18in. tall. Leaves stiff and flattened, somewhat fibrous.

Found in moist meadows and woodlands, and on water margins throughout the USA, except in the Pacific states, and in southern Canada.

There are several other Blue-eyed Grasses, none as widespread as this species but a similar one is found in the Pacific states. They differ mainly in the width and texture of the leaves, and many have unbranched flower stalks. Some have white or yellow flowers.

Flowering period: March–June.

Other Common Species

Common Skullcap (1) Hairy creeping stems with erect, leafy branches. Solitary two-lipped flowers in axils. Wet meadows, marshes throughout.

Blue Gilia (2) Erect plant, with finely divided leaves & terminal balls of flowers. Grassy slopes, W USA & Can.

Wild Hyacinth (3) Corm with a few grass-like leaves. Flowers tubular, in loose umbels at top of leafless stalk. Plains & hillsides, SW & W USA.

Lyre-leaved Sage (4) Lyre-shaped leaves in rosette with erect, branched spike of two-lipped flowers in whorls. Open ground, roadsides E & SE USA.

Blue Flag (5) Thick underground stem produces sword-shaped leaves & stems with several flowers. Wet meadows, marshes C & W USA & W Can.

Single flowers grow on long flower stalks in the leaf axils, opening only in sun. Petals five, bright red, joined at the base and falling as one unit. Fruits are rounded capsules cupped by sepals.

A small hairless annual weed with many branched prostrate stems, often rooting at the nodes and forming a small spreading mat. Leaves opposite, small, ovate and stalkless.

Found in lawns and on cultivated land, in waste ground and on roadsides throughout the USA and southern Canada.

Scarlet Pimpernel is not likely to be confused with other plants for no other weed has such simple, solitary bright red flowers. Moneywort is a larger species from the same family that grows in wet ground and has yellow flowers.

Flowering period: March–November. (P) March–July.

Flowers in widely separated whorls on 12in. tall erect stems. Calyx tubular, with dense white hairs, flowers reddish-purple, hooded and tubular with spotted lower lip. Fruits are nutlets, in fours, in persistent calyxes.

Annual plant with hairy, four-angled stems, often lax with many branches and rooting at the nodes. Leaves opposite, rounded with scalloped edges, lower ones with long stalks but uppermost clasping the stem.

Found in waste places, on roadsides, in lawns and fields throughout the USA and in southern Canada. European alien.

Red Dead-nettle is very similar but has toothed, arrow-shaped leaves and flowers in dense flower spikes. Hedge-nettles are also similar but their leaves are more lance-shaped and the lower lips of their flowers are obviously three-lobed.

Flowering period: March–November. (P) March–August.

Flowers small, pale pink, with five separate, notched petals; borne on short stalks in two clusters in the axils of the upper leaves. Cranesbill fruit is distinctive, like a five-part beak which splits into spoon-shaped sections.

An annual plant, up to 15in. tall, with a clump of long-stalked, palmate, deeply divided basal leaves and several freely branched, densely hairy stems. Stem leaves similar to basal leaves.

Found in dry open grassy places, meadows and waste ground, as well as on roadsides and in yards, throughout the USA and southern Canada.

There are several other cranesbills widespread in N. America, including the perennial Richardson's Cranesbill, a western species with larger pink, purple-veined flowers and Bicknell's Cranesbill with small magenta flowers borne in twos.

Flowering period: April–August.

92

Bull Thistle (1), Canada Thistle (2)

Flower head composed of a bristly, rounded "base" supporting a dense cluster of mauve to red-purple, tubular florets; heads solitary or in clusters at top of stem. Seeds have feathery or simple hairs.

Spiny annual, biennial or perennial plants with erect stems, usually between 2 and 4ft. tall; and alternately arranged, deeply toothed or divided, spine-tipped leaves. Some species have spiny stems, in others the stems are spineless.

Found in waste places and on roadsides, in fields and pastures throughout the USA and Canada. Some of the most common are European aliens.

Amongst the most common are Bull Thistle; Canada Thistle which forms spreading colonies; and Musk Thistle, a very spiny species with spiky bracts beneath the nodding flower heads. Burdocks have hooked flower "bases" which form burrs. **Knapweeds** are not spiny.

Flowering period: June–September.

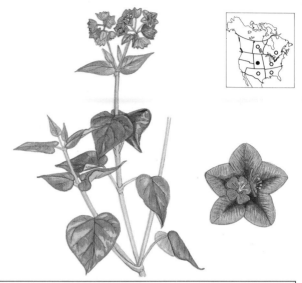

Flowers distinctive, cup-shaped, with no petals but five purple, united sepals; borne in clusters of two or three in a five-lobed, dish-shaped bract in the upper leaf axils. Fruits five-angled, densely hairy, in enlarged bracts.

A large perennial plant, up to 6ft. tall, with many thick, forked stems growing from the crown. Stems are swollen at the nodes and the large opposite leaves are fleshy and heart-shaped.

Found on the prairies and on roadsides and railroad embankments in central and eastern USA but less common in the east; also found in central southern Canada.

There are other Four o'clock species including an annual garden species which may become naturalized in the south. This has turban-like bracts and funnel-shaped flowers in a variety of colors. In the west there are other species with white or pink bell-shaped or funnel-shaped flowers.

Flowering period: May–September.

FIREWEED ☀▲

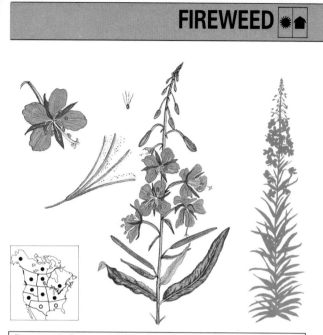

Rosy purple flowers with four petals, borne in large terminal flowering spikes. Flower buds droop before opening. Seed capsules erect, up to 3in. long, split longitudinally to release many feathery seeds.

A perennial plant with widely spreading roots, from which grow large numbers of tall erect leafy stems. Leaves are long and narrow, dark green and angled upwards, alternate or spirally arranged on the stems.

Often forms wide colonies in woodland clearings and on disturbed ground, especially after fire. Throughout the USA and Canada, in mountain areas in south.

Distinguished from other common Willow-herbs, like Hairy Willow-herb and Purple-leaved Willow-herb, by its flowers which grow horizontally instead of pointing upwards. It may also be confused with **Purple Loosestrife**, but the flowers of this plant have six petals.

Flowering period: July–September.

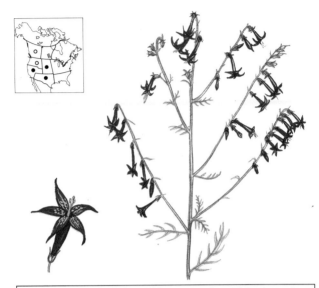

Flowers long and tubular with long pointed petal-lobes becoming reflexed when older, red in color and often with yellow spots; borne in clusters in the leaf axils of the uppermost leaves. Fruits are capsules.

A biennial or perennial plant, 2–3ft. tall, with an erect, often branched, sticky-hairy stem, and narrowly dissected leaves divided into narrow "leaflets".

Found in open, dry sandy and rocky places and grassland in southern, western and central USA and B.C. but not in the rest of Canada.

This plant belongs to the same family as the **Phloxes**, the **Gilias** and the Linanthuses; many of these are western species, like the Skyrocket, and many have pink flowers. Others have white flowers. Linanthuses have distinctive, stalkless leaves, palmately divided into narrow segments.

Flowering period: June–September.

GAYFEATHERS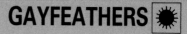

Dotted Gayfeather

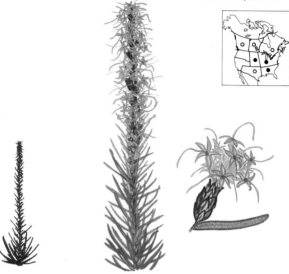

Flower heads pinkish purple, formed from tubular florets only, borne in crowded spikes at the tops of the erect stems. They open from the top of the spike downwards. Seeds bear slender feathery hairs.

Perennial plants with several erect stems, bearing many crowded, alternately arranged, simple leaves. These leaves are often covered with glandular dots, especially in the species illustrated.

Most are found in dry open places and dry prairies, a few in moist ground, in central and eastern USA and Canada but not west of the Rocky Mountains.

There are several prairie species of Gayfeathers, including Dotted Gayfeather, which is found in dry areas and Prairie Gayfeather which grows in damp prairies; Dense Gayfeather is a more easterly species of wet meadows and wet open woods. These plants are often also called Blazing Stars.

Flowering period: August–October.

Flowers borne in threes, on long flower stalks which have tufts of leaves half-way up. Flowers purplish or paler, vase-shaped and nodding, with five petals. Seeds of seed-head have very long feathery plumes.

A softly hairy perennial plant, up to 18in. tall, with a clump of pinnate leaves. Leaves have 9–19 opposite, jagged leaflets, some much larger than others.

Found in prairie grassland and in dry open areas in prairie and foothill regions throughout much of N. America except the southeast.

One of several Avens species found in N. America, all clump-forming plants with irregular pinnate leaves. Yellow Avens is a woodland plant with clusters of small yellow flowers on tall flower stalks; Water Avens has pinkish brown nodding flowers. Both have distinctive clusters of hooked fruits.

Flowering period: May–June.

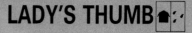

Knotweed (1)

Flowers pink, borne in tight spikes, often with a single leaf at the base of the spike. The pink color of the flowers comes from the sepals, for petals are absent. Brown, shining fruits are borne in similar spikes.

A spreading annual plant, with several smooth reddish stems. Swellings above the nodes give the stems an angular appearance. Leaves alternate, lance-shaped, with distinctive fringed leaf sheaths at their bases.

Found in waste places and cultivated ground, especially where the land is wet where it may reach up to 24in. tall, throughout the USA and Canada.

There are many similar species. Pale Smartweed has green stems, leaf-sheaths without fringes and greenish-white flowers; Knotweed (inset) is a common weed with small bluish leaves, silvery leaf-sheaths and tiny white or green flowers.

Flowering period: June–frost.

Flowers immediately recognizable, with backwardly pointing spurs on all five red petals and a long column of yellow stamens; nodding on long stems on branches of the flowering stalks. Fruits are clusters of erect pods.

A perennial plant which forms a basal clump of long-stalked, distinctively divided leaves with lobed leaflets in threes, and a few taller flowering stems, 2–3ft. high. Stem leaves become progressively smaller and simpler towards the top.

Found in damp woodland and in moist and rocky places, along streams and in meadows in central and eastern areas of the USA and Canada.

A similar species is found in the Pacific states and in western and northern Canada, but its flowers are red and yellow and are produced slightly later. Other columbine species have yellow, white or blue flowers. **Delphinium** flowers only have a single spur.

Flowering period: March–June.

CARDINAL FLOWER

Stiffly upright, leafy flowering stems are unbranched with many distinctive, bright red flowers growing in a dense spike at the top. Fruits are rounded capsules cupped by sepals and opening by pores.

A perennial, succulent plant with basal rosettes of lance-shaped, toothed leaves from which grow offshoots, smaller rosettes which may form separate plants. Erect leafy flowering spikes grow up to 4ft. tall.

Found in wet meadows and woods, along the sides of streams and in marshes, in southern and eastern areas of the USA, including Calif. and southeastern Canada.

There are no other plants quite like this! There are other Lobelias but they generally have blue or white flowers.

Flowering period: July–October.

Flowers highly distinctive, like small shooting stars with five pink or white petals completely reflexed and a column of stamens extending forward; borne in a nodding cluster terminating the flowering stem. Fruits are capsules.

A small perennial plant with a rosette of large, paddle-shaped, usually hairless leaves, each up to one foot long and one or a few leafless flowering stems.

There are several similar species found in moist woodland, meadows and prairies, spreading throughout the USA and Canada between them, but more common in the west.

The Shooting Star species vary mainly in the color of their flowers, from deep magenta to pale pink and white. They cannot be mistaken for any other wildflowers

Flowering period: April–July, but varying with species.

NORTHERN GENTIAN

Flowers often numerous, usually pink-purple but may be blue or white, vase-shaped with five petal lobes and facing upwards; borne in clusters in the axils of the leaves. Fruits are dry cylindrical capsules.

An annual or biennial plant, up to 18in. tall, with a basal clump of oval leaves and a few stiff, upright, leafy stems, often branched and the branches angled upwards. Stem leaves opposite, lance-shaped and stalkless.

Found in moist places in meadows and woods, also amongst wet rocks and gravels throughout Canada, in western USA especially in the mountains and in northeastern USA.

This species, one of the commonest of the gentians, can be distinguished by the color of its flowers; the others have deep blue blooms. Fringed Gentians are relatively common and have only four petal-lobes, with fringed edges. Other species are more restricted in their distribution.

Flowering period: June–September.

Other Common Species

Storksbill (1) Lacy leaves in rosettes. Flowers in small clusters on long stalks. Fruits like storks' bills. Roadsides, lawns throughout.

Tick Trefoil (2) Erect stem with whorl of leaves, each with 3 leaflets. Flowers pea-like. Pods segmented. Woods C & E USA & Can.

Everlasting Pea (3) Smooth scrambling plant with winged stems. Leaves with 2 leaflets & one tendril. Flowers like sweet peas. Roadsides E & W.

Knapweed (4) Clump of branched stems with pinnate leaves and flower heads on long stalks. Outer florets divided. Fields, roadsides. E, rarer in W & C.

Purple Loosestrife (5) Erect 4-angled stems with narrow leaves & 6-petaled flowers in axils. Damp ground. C & E USA & S Can.

Other Common Species

Farewell-to-Spring (1) Erect stems with narrow, upwardly pointing leaves. Large open flowers crowded near top of stem. Pacific coast.

Corncockle (2) Erect plant with narrow, opposite leaves. Terminal flowers in calyx with 5 long, narrow lobes. Woods, grain fields throughout.

Fairy Slipper (3) One broad, long-stalked leaf and one stem bearing a drooping flower with 4 petals and slipperlike lip. Damp woods. Can. & N USA.

Spreading Dogbane (4) Erect spreading plant with simple opposite leaves & milky sap. Flowers in terminal clusters. Woods throughout.

Meadow Rue (5) Clump of leaves with leaflets in 3s. Flowers have purple-green sepals & yellow stamens. Damp woods, meadows. S Can. & N USA.

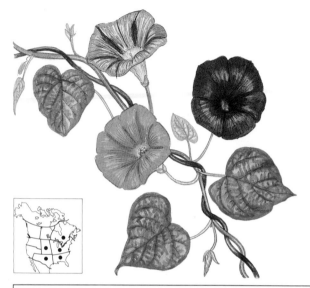

Flowers funnel-shaped, up to 3in. long, blue, purple or pink, borne in small clusters of up to five blossoms on short stalks in the axils of the leaves. Fruits are rounded capsules, enclosed in persistent sepals.

An annual twining plant with several stems, covered with soft hairs and bearing alternate, heart-shaped leaves. The familiar Morning Glory grown in gardens.

Found on roadsides and waste places, in fields and thickets throughout much of the USA except the Pacific states, and in southeastern Canada.

This is one of several Morning Glories, grown in gardens, to have become naturalized. Native species include Ivy-leaved Morning Glory which has three-lobed leaves; and Beach Morning Glory with kidney-shaped leaves, common on Calif. beaches.

Flowering period: July–frost.

Hedge Bindweed (1), Field Bindweed (2)

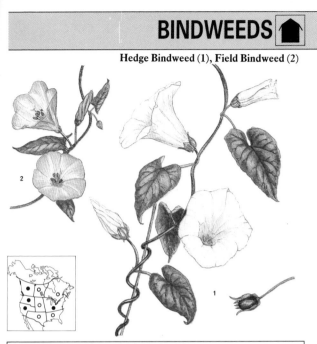

Bindweeds have funnel-shaped flowers growing in the leaf axils. The white flowers of Hedge Bindweed grow singly and are 2in. long; those of Field Bindweed are pink, about one inch long and may grow in ones or pairs.

These two troublesome weeds are perennial twining vines with deep spreading roots which can penetrate 3ft. into the ground. Their smooth arrow-shaped leaves are larger in Hedge Bindweed (up to 5in. long).

Both are found scattered throughout the USA and southern Canada on roadsides, in waste places and thickets but Hedge Bindweed generally grows in wetter places. European aliens.

Several related species grow in dry areas in Calif. and Oregon. These include the Sierra Morning Glory which is a trailing species covered with fine hairs; and the Western Morning Glory which is a tall climbing plant with sharp-pointed leaves.

Flowering period: May–September.

✸⌂CLOVERS

White Clover (1), Red Clover (2)

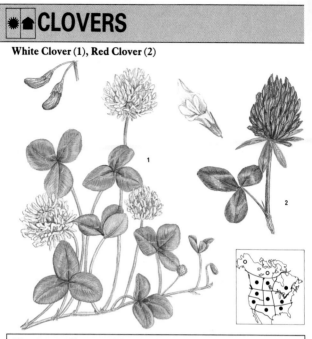

Flowers pea-like, purplish red or white often tinged with pink and with abundant nectar at the base of the tube, borne in tight heads on long stalks in leaf axils. Fruits are small pods enclosed in dead persistent flowers.

Perennial plants, only about 6in. high, with many thin creeping stems rooting at the nodes. Leaves with three leaflets, in some species with a distinctive pale crescentic band around the base of each leaflet.

Common plants of grassy places and roadsides throughout the USA and Canada and may be troublesome weeds in lawns. Some of the most common are European aliens.

There are many Clovers of which by far the most common are White Clover and Red Clover, both with similar crescentic marks on their leaves. Alsike Clover has plain unmarked leaflets and pinkish-white flowers.

Flowering period: April–October.

WILD BUCKWHEATS ☀

Umbrella-plant (1), Nodding Buckwheat (2)

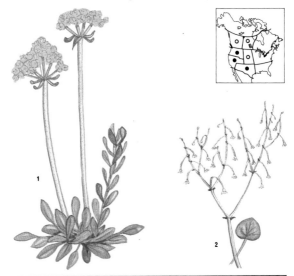

Flowers white, yellow or pink, often tinged with green; color provided by the six sepals, no petals. Borne in umbels or on long stalks in loose clusters, terminating erect flowering stalks. Fruits three-angled or three-winged.

Small annual or perennial plants with basal rosettes of simple leaves, often covered with dense white hairs either on the upper or lower surface, or all over. Flowers borne on erect flowering stalks.

The majority of species are found in dry stony places in the Rocky Mountains and in the western deserts but a few grow in dry ground in the prairies of the USA and Canada.

A very large group of plants related to the Cultivated Buckwheat, an erect leafy plant with arrow-shaped leaves and clusters of pink flowers which is sometimes found on roadsides and waste ground in the east. The related **Lady's Thumb** and **Knotweed** are common weeds.

Flowering period: May–August, depending on species.

☀ PHACELIAS

Wild Heliotrope (1), Miami Mist (2)

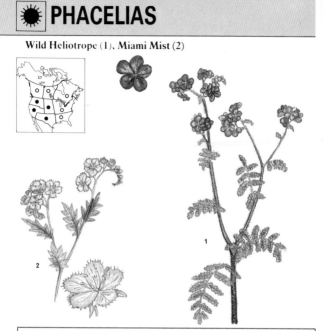

Flowers may be numerous and showy or fewer and less noticeable, blue or white, bell-shaped or saucer-shaped; borne in curled, one-sided clusters terminating the stems. Fruits are capsules.

Hairy annual to perennial plants, up to 3ft. tall but mostly smaller, forming a clump of erect or sprawling leafy stems. Leaves usually alternate, usually pinnate or deeply divided, but in some species only toothed or lobed.

The great majority of this large group of plants are found in western USA, usually in dry places, desert and scrub areas. Most eastern species grow in woods and meadows.

Wild Heliotrope is one of many southwestern Phacelias found in fields and deserts. Miami Mist is a southeastern species and can be recognized by its distinctive pale blue, fringed petals. Several Canadian and mid-western species have been given the name Scorpion Weeds.

Flowering period: March–June.

Hairy Rock Cress (1), Spreading Rock Cress (2)

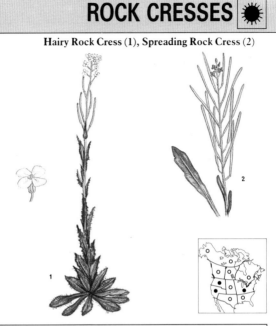

Flowers white or purple, with four petals in the form of a cross; borne on erect flowering stalks, the lowermost opening first and the stalk lengthening as the season progresses. Fruits are long upright or curved pods.

Biennial or perennial plants with basal rosettes of leaves, usually simple and entire but toothed in some species, and erect leafy flower stems, up to 3ft. tall but smaller in many species. Some are hairless, while others are hairy.

Found on the slopes of mountains and foothills, as well as in prairies and woodland throughout the USA and Canada. Many are high mountain species.

Rock Cresses are generally identified by the form of their pods. Most grow in only a small area but a few are more widespread. Hairy Rock Cress grows on slopes, in woods and prairies throughout N. America except the south. Spreading Rock Cress is a mountain species of the west and north.

Flowering period: May–July.

111

Milkvetch (1), Alpine Locoweed (2)

Flowers pea-like, white, yellow or purple in color, borne in long spikes in the leaf axils. Pods variable but often divided into two compartments.

Most milkvetches are perennial clump-forming plants with many erect stems bearing pinnate leaves. The leaves have many opposite leaflets and one terminal leaflet. Many species are covered with downy hairs.

Many grow on dry stony hillsides and flats and in dry grassland, especially in the west where most species are found, but others grow in moist ground and beside streams.

There are two groups of plants found throughout most of North America, known variously as Milkvetches or **Locoweeds**, some of which are poisonous to stock. Both illustrated species are widely distributed, Milkvetch in woods and beside streams and Alpine Locoweed in mountain woodland.

Flowering period: May–September.

MILKWEEDS ☀:’

Butterfly Weed (1), Showy Milkweed (2)

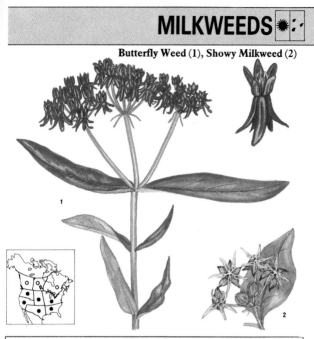

Flowers borne in umbels, either terminally or in leaf axils.
Flowers unmistakable, the stamens forming a structure like a
crown, with five turned-back petals. Seed pods often cigar-shaped
or narrower, with feathery seeds.

Erect perennial plants, usually with a single stem which may or
may not be branched and thick milky sap. Leaves usually large,
opposite or in whorls, simple, linear, lance-shaped or ovate in
shape, often with white downy hairs.

Found mostly in open woodland or on dry open ground. A few
species grow in wet places. Most are found in southern and central
USA but some grow throughout.

Amongst the most common are Butterfly Weed with red or yellow
flowers and Common Milkweed with white or pink flowers; both
grow on roadsides and in dry fields. Showy Milkweed is a western
dry ground species with creamy flowers. Whorled Milkweed
grows in open woods.

Flowering period: May–August.

113

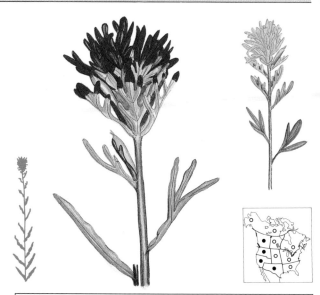

Flowers borne in dense spikes on the tops of the stems. Bright red or yellow leaf-like bracts in the flower spike give it its color. Flowers are tubular, dull green or yellow. Fruits are capsules.

Perennial, clump-forming, downy plants with several erect stems, usually between 1ft. and 3ft. tall. Leaves alternately arranged on the stem, the lower ones simple, the upper ones often three-lobed.

Most species grow on dry open ground in western USA and Canada on both sides of the Rocky Mountains. Some grow in woods and meadows and a few are found in the east.

There are very many Indian Paintbrushes, with bracts varying in color from red as in the featured plant, to yellow-bracted plants and orange. Few are widespread. One species is found in woods and on roadsides in eastern and central N. America but this is not found in the west where the majority grow.

Flowering period: May–August.

BEARDSTONGUES ☀:

Slender Blue Beardstongue (1), Foxglove Beardstongue (2)

The clusters of purple, blue, white or red, showy flowers are borne on pairs of long stalks, growing from opposite leaf axils. Each is tubular with a hairy sterile stamen in the throat, hence the name. Fruits are capsules.

A very varied group of perennial plants, ranging from tall, clump-forming grassland species to cushion-forming mountain species. Their simple leaves are arranged in opposite pairs, are often without stalks and may be toothed.

Found in a variety of habitats, from prairies to woods to open mountain ledges throughout N. America, but many more are present in the USA than in Canada.

Slender Blue Beardstongue is a widespread prairie species while the Foxglove Beardstongue is more common in damp fields and roadsides in central and eastern USA. The largest number of Beardstongues are found in the west on both sides of the Rocky Mountains as well as in them.

Flowering period: June–August.

Early Blue, Yellow Prairie, Wild White Violets

Early flowers distinctive, with five petals and a spur at the back; blue-violet, white or yellow. They grow on long stalks, directly from the crown or in leaf axils, depending on species. Later flowers do not open but produce capsules.

Small, usually perennial, plants either with several branched stems or with the leaves and flowers all growing from a central crown. Leaves are often toothed, usually have long stalks and may be rounded, divided or lobed.

There are very many violets in N. America, both rare and common, mostly growing in damp places, in woods and meadows, especially in mountain areas in the south.

Early Blue Violet, together with many other violet-flowered species, is widespread in open woods and damp meadows across the continent. White violets are less common; Wild White Violet grows in northern states and Canada, in mountains in the south. Yellow violets are more common in the west.

Flowering period: April–July.

116

Wake Robin (1), Nodding Trillium (2)

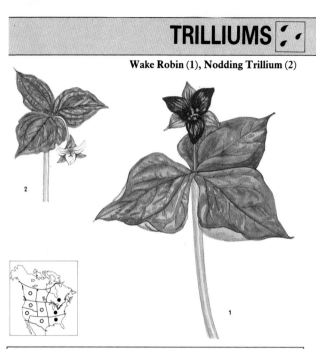

The solitary flower is borne in the center of the three leaves; it may be white or red-purple, borne on a stalk or stalkless, depending on species. Fruit is a round red-purple berry with many seeds.

Perennial plants with short, thick underground stems, from which grow erect stems, up to 18in. tall, each terminated by a whorl of three broad, pointed leaves often mottled with green or purple, and one flower.

Most species are found in moist woods in eastern USA and southeast Canada, a few in mountain areas in the Pacific states.

Nodding Trillium and White Trillium are amongst the commonest of the white-flowered species. Wake Robin is the most common of the red-flowered species. Toad-shade and Prairie Trillium have flowers with erect, not spreading, petals. All these are eastern species.

Flowering period: April–June.

Northern Green Orchid (1), Tall White Orchid (2)

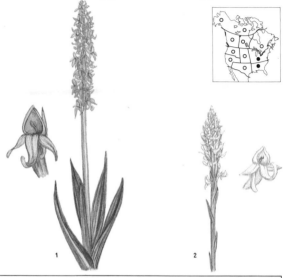

Many green or white, often fragrant flowers, borne in a dense spike at the top of the flowering shoot. Each flower has four lateral "petals", another at the back and a lip which is extended to form a spur.

Stout perennial plants with a single erect flowering shoot, up to 3ft. tall, bearing many long, sheathing leaves especially near the base. Upper leaves much smaller than lower ones.

Bog Orchids are found in moist woods, meadows and bogs throughout the USA and Canada. Northern Green Orchid grows only in the northern parts of this area.

Bracted Orchid has leaf-like bracts in the flower spike. Several Bog Orchids have white flowers, like Tall White Orchid, One-leaved Rein Orchid and Round-leaved Orchid. Many eastern Bog Orchids have fringed flower lips and are known as Fringed Orchids.

Flowering period: (S) May–July. (N) June–August.

Flowers nodding, funnel-shaped at first, then petals reflexed; borne on a long stalk growing from between the two leaves. Yellow, or creamy white and yellow on inside. Fruit a more or less oblong capsule.

A perennial plant, producing one or two lance-shaped leaves each spring, from deeply buried corms and often spreading by offshoots. Leaves often mottled with brown marks.

Found in woods especially in central and eastern USA and southeast Canada. Often grown in gardens.

White Dog-tooth Violet is most common in central USA, yellow Dog-tooth Violet in the east. There are several other white or cream-flowered Dog-tooth Violets, some with several flowers to one stem, which grow in the southwest USA, where they are often called Adder's Tongues.

Flowering period: April–May.

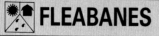

Common Fleabane (1), Daisy Fleabane (2)

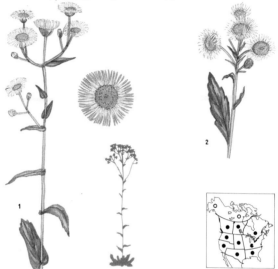

Daisy-like flower heads are solitary or borne in branched clusters at the tops of the stems. Flower heads have many white, blue or pink ray florets and a large yellow disk. Seeds have slender hairs.

Annual or perennial plants, often with basal leaf rosettes. Flower-bearing stems erect, with alternate, simple leaves or leafless. Some species are covered with fine dense hairs, others hairless.

Found in woods and pastures, on roadsides and waste places throughout the USA and Canada. There are also many mountain species.

Unlike the **Asters**, which they resemble, Fleabanes bloom in spring and early summer. A common roadside species is Daisy Fleabane with white flowers; Common Fleabane grows in moist woods and meadows; Blue Fleabane is found in northern USA and Canada.

Flowering period: April–July.

Smooth Aster (1), Heath Aster (2)

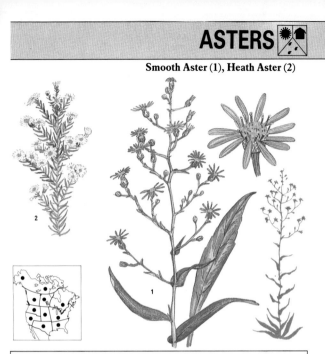

Flowers with blue, pink or white ray florets around red, yellow or white disks; borne in branching clusters or sprays at the tops of the stems or in upper leaf axils. Seeds bear barbed hairs.

Perennial plants with leafy, upright or weakly erect stems, growing from creeping stems or forming a clump. Leaves alternate, simple, with smooth or toothed margins.

Found in a variety of habitats from open woods and dry open ground, to moist meadows, marshes and salt-marshes throughout the USA and southern Canada.

There are very many Asters, most of them local to a small area. Widespread species include Smooth Aster which grows on woodland edges; Western Willow Aster, with white or pinkish-blue flowers, which grows beside streams and ditches; and Heath Aster (inset), which grows in open sandy places.

Flowering period: August–October.

121

Index and Check-list

All species in roman type are illustrated
Keep a record of your sightings by checking the boxes